FENG SHUI
for
ARCHITECTURE

FENG SHUI
for
ARCHITECTURE

How to Design, Build and Remodel to
Create a Healthy and Serene Home

SIMONA F. MAININI, Dr. Arch.

Library of Congress Number: 2003094574
ISBN :   Hardcover   1-4134-1961-5
                    Softcover   1-4134-1960-7

To order additional copies of this book, contact:
Xlibris Corporation
1-888-795-4274
www.Xlibris.com
Orders@Xlibris.com
19673

This book is dedicated to . . .

my parents, Tilde and Francesco, without whom neither
I or this book would never have existed,

and my mentor, Master 'Sifu' Sang, who had confidence
in my skills and my positive attitude and found me
fit to become his trusted student,

and Michael and Raphaelle Tamura, who encouraged me
to take up the pen and gave me a lot of "spiritual space"
while rearranging the furniture in their house.

To all of you, thank you.

CONTENTS

Feng Shui in Wind and Water Patterns
Feng = Wind
Shui = Water

Urban Environments and Manmade Structures
Buildings as Mountains
Roads as Water Courses

Garden Purpose and Style
Landscape Design Considerations
Garden "No-Nos"

Trees and Plants
Correcting Lot Shape and Creating the Armchair
Protection from Inauspicious Sha
Planning Ahead
Unfavorable Landscape Conditions

Fountains and Pools
Water and Qi
Shape and Size of Water Features
A Cautionary Note

Garden Timing
Weak Areas to Avoid

Sha and the Five Elements
Fire Sha
Metal Sha

CHAPTER 8

Simona Mainini has been a dedicated student of mine since 1996. She has taken every class that we have offered, completed our instructor training, and has been very active in our American Society of Feng Shui.

Simona has also assisted me in Feng Shui readings. She displays bright talent, both in design and in Feng Shui ability. She is always hard working, diligent, and creative.

Feng Shui for Architecture is an excellent guide for both the Feng Shui professional and layperson. Now, you can benefit from the knowledge presented here and can adjust your environment to make it as harmonious as possible.

It is with great pleasure that I write this introduction for my student. I have confidence in the results of her endeavors.

Master Larry Sang, President and Founder
The American Feng Shui Institute

Forward to *Feng Shui For Architecture*

As more of our clients become aware of the impact of their surroundings, our design of their homes has also become more sophisticated. As architects, we have become intimately aware that our surroundings affect how we think, feel and act. It therefore comes as no surprise that the science and art of Feng Shui has experienced a tremendous growth among homebuyers. We are all searching for a way to reduce stress, create harmony, and find inner peace in our professional and personal lives. The answer may lie within this clearly written book.

Although Feng Shui has its roots in ancient Chinese history, modern masters such as Simona Mainini have been instrumental in applying these principles to our built environment. These Feng Shui principles are constant and apply both at home and at the office. It is important to know that they exist on the empty lot before the new house is built, and it's important to know that the design of the house can amplify or minimize these forces.

With her book, *Feng Shui for Architecture*, Ms. Mainini has finally filled a gap. She has taken the rather complicated subject of Feng Shui as it applies to architecture and she has successfully laid out a step-by-step guide to understanding the mysteries of this ancient art.

Our association with Ms. Mainini has been incredibly educational. We initially worked with her to develop a custom residence in Northern California. She guided us each step of the way. Her initial analysis of possible building sites lead to the selection of a lot that was ideally suited to the client. Our great challenge was to develop a plan that reflected Ms. Mainini's concerns for all phases of their lives: health, wealth, emotional, creativity and harmony. The resulting floor plan was a marriage of good architectural design that reflected the specific needs of our client and considered those Feng Shui principles that were specific to them. We learned that it was possible to blend the unique requirements that Simona had established as necessary for our client's welfare with good architecture. The solution was a classic design that will perfectly match the needs of our clients.

This book is a step-by-step guide, with examples, to help you select the site, develop the floor plan and, bring in colors and materials that are compatible with you or your client. Ms. Mainini has done an exemplary job of keeping this very complicated subject clear and concise for the layperson.

As people discover that these principles of nature are indisputable and that they affect us both at work and at home, masters of the art and science of Feng Shui such as Simona Mainini will continue to enrich our lives in ways we could only have imagined.

Brian Dawson, AIA
Dawson Hannouche Partners, Architecture Planning
Newport Beach, CA

Introduction to *Feng Shui for Architecture*

This book is a guide to using the ancient science and philosophy of *Feng Shui* for the purpose of designing, building, remodeling, and decorating our homes successfully. The information is presented in a user-friendly manual format and can be utilized by homeowners, builders and professional designers and architects.

When first introduced to Feng Shui, most people ask, "Should I wait until after the building is designed, constructed, and decorated and have it all in nice shape, or should I work with a Feng Shui expert before I start all this?"

Some may think that by calling in a Feng Shui expert after everything is completed and seems perfect, things will more likely look complete and perfect to the Feng Shui master as well. This is usually not so.

I like to make my clients feel comfortable with their efforts and their homes, but I believe that when they hire me, they also expect me to give them advice on how to make their homes more favorable places to live. Of course, I prefer being able to communicate with them ahead of time, when they can make the big changes that make the big differences. That is one of the main reasons that this book, which has been swirling around in my head for years, came about: to assist homeowners and professionals in designing houses with "good" Feng Shui from the start instead of trying to put a bandage on problems or make patchwork corrections after the fact.

The idea here is to do it right from the start, while you're still sketching your ideas on paper. This way, after all the madness of the designing, building, and decorating is over, when you turn to ask the Feng Shui master, "How did I do?" the answer will be, "Very well, my friend!" rather than, "Pretty good, but . . ."

The Origins of My Calling

As a child in Italy, I grew up reading Asian fairy tales about wise men and virtuous, deity-like women. These people seemed to know the secrets of the universe: happiness, peace and serenity, and at the end of the story they always unveiled a precious moral, at times different from those in Western fairy tales. This is not generally the model that most Western youth are brought up with, but it worked pretty well for me and it was what made those men and women so wise in my estimation. Little did I realize that one day I would come face to face with such esteemed men.

In those days, I also remember being very sensitive to the "energies" around me. Since my parents were involved in an interior design and modern-Italian-furniture retail business, they very much enjoyed collecting antique furnishings; it was their hobby and our home contained several pieces from previous centuries. I, however, wasn't interested in their antiques.

All I saw was a sort of 'gray cloud' around those pieces and, if I got too close to them, my vision would become blurry. It also made me think of the people who had owned them through all those centuries; they brought back memories of eras that were long past, before I was even born.

It was so different with the new furniture we sold in our store; those pieces were sparkling, shiny and "clear." I felt good when sitting on a new chair or sofa—I could think more clearly, I did my homework much more easily, and I could focus on my life and my friends, rather than on someone else who had been gone for centuries.

With the passage of years and an art-school education, I came to understand what my parents saw in the antiques; the beauty of the designs that had lasted for centuries. Still, I made up my mind that when I had my own space, I would own only new furniture, straight from the factory and therefore not owned by someone else, because my sense of well-being was most important to me, while those antiques didn't feel quite right.

An Architect's Journey

Immersed in an atmosphere of design and home furnishings, by the time I got to university I had a very clear idea of how an ideal residential building should be designed.

Throughout art school and architecture school, I became familiar with fashionable trends and originality in design.

During these years, I also traveled throughout Asia. While visiting Japan I observed the cultural details and designs with enchanted eyes. European architects have been attracted to Japanese design ever since they have been able to travel to the Far East. They have tried, to the best of their capabilities, to imitate the Japanese attention to construction detail – a beam, a post, the patina of the materials, sliding doors leading from a building into the garden, the simple elegance of the design and the superb play of light and shade. As an architect-to-be, I was swept off my feet by it all.

While I was visiting Hong Kong, our tour guide continually praised the expertise of their Feng Shui masters: apparently no custom home, no corporate building, no commercial investment was even planned without first consulting one of these experts. When it was requested that he elaborate on what such a master might do, the guide would mumble elusively, "It's a Chinese secret."

For several weeks after returning to Italy, I tried to introduce some of the same elements into my designs. Curiously, I couldn't get the same effect and neither have many of the other European architects who have tried. No matter how beautiful their creations may have been, the innate sense of balance and harmony of their Asian counterparts was missing.

As I later discovered, Feng Shui isn't limited strictly to Hong Kong, Taiwan and other locations in countries throughout Asia each have their own versions of Feng Shui. I started wondering if these "Chinese secrets" were behind the sense of peace, stability, and harmony I was experiencing through my rudimentary and yet consistent sensitivity to the energies around me.

I went on to complete my training at the School of Architecture at Milan's Polytechnic University. I learned about the history of art and architecture, practical information about building construction, architectural design and planning. I also learned more about the so-called "ritual and spiritual" practices of architectural design in Asia, or at least what was available to Westerners back then.

For years, I witnessed an ongoing debate about style and functionality, which has permeated the history of architecture. Was one more important than the other? For me, the question was not whether one was better then the other; ideally, I wanted to have both. Nevertheless, I still had a question:

> Is it necessary for architecture to be based on style and functionality alone, or could there exist something more fundamental that influences our lives and experiences?

It seemed to me that while style, good taste, and functionality were fine on a basic aesthetic and practical level, they did not always reach the goal of ensuring the inhabitants of happiness, decent lives, and overall well-being. Some remarkable examples of great design have, after all, also been the settings for the unfortunate experiences of many families. Something was clearly missing.

The Missing Link

The first hint of that "missing something" came in a university physics class, when my professor detoured from his regular lecture on thermodynamics and building insulation in order to shed light on developments in modern physics that sounded more like *meta*physics:

Mechanistic physics is quickly being replaced by quantum physics. This means that instead of a world of "stuff," we have a world of invisible energy, made visible through its interaction with our own energy systems. Our entire universe, which we know through a well-established series of reference systems, may have more laws of physics than those we are acquainted with. If so, our current reference system may need to be revised and updated. What we perceive as chaos today may in fact be an order that we do not yet know how to interpret. Once we find these laws, chaos will become a well-defined reality with causes and effects.

What we commonly acknowledge as a universe made of physical matter contains in reality about the same quantity of "stuff" as grapefruit. If we look deeply into every object, we see not matter but an interchange of energetically balanced and opposing polarities: a world of electrons, protons, and neutrons rhythmically dancing around each other. All physical matter dances to different rhythms: the electrons and protons and neutrons of your hand dance to a different rhythm than those in your desk. And this is the main reason why your "end" doesn't go through the desk but rather remains on its surface. Different rhythms are easy to recognize because they look, feel, taste, and smell different to our senses. What we define as the input of the five senses is actually our body's energy rhythm clashing with the energy rhythm of the object we are observing as we interact with our five senses.

This is a fairly new field for modern science, and we do not yet know completely how it works. The only thing that seems clear so far is that the entire universe may be organized this way. In other words, energy may be made of different polarities holding together a very limited amount of matter. It may even be possible that this energy follows certain patterns of transformation that make it shift from one frequency to another and therefore changes its status in the physical world.

Is there any form of intelligence guiding it? Is there any rational plan behind it? Can chaos be explained using laws and rules? What is the common link that holds this physical universe together? And, of course, the ultimate question is WHY?

I found all this fascinating. Now that I am more aware of the incredible tapestry of the connection relating science, nature, and the divine, I realize that they are all part of the same whole.

I also came to realize why the greatest architects of the past, such as Michelangelo, Borromini, Bernini and Guarino Guarini, to mention just a few, had pursued the study of metaphysics. I suspect they, too, were searching for an "invisible ideal" order of design and ultimately of life.

Junior Organic Architect

Shortly after my graduation from the Milan Polytechnic's School of Architecture, I embarked on an internship with the Eric Lloyd Wright architectural firm in Los Angeles, California. There, I became well acquainted with many architects who were following the principles of organic architecture introduced by Frank Lloyd Wright. I also had the chance of visiting most of the wonderful structures based on these principles that had proliferated throughout this bustling metropolis.

Much to my surprise, there weren't any codified rules for practicing organic architecture, in fact, much of the Organic Architectural practice hinged on the designer's intuitive interpretation. I found myself becoming increasingly aware of the tremendous influence the Asian culture had on this organic concept of architecture in the United States, as it had had in Europe, and the respect and admiration modern organic architects have for it.

Frank Lloyd Wright himself, I was told, had been a great admirer of the Taoist philosopher Lao Tzu. He had read his writings extensively and had tried to incorporate these principles of nature in his own designs. He also traveled in Asia and probably became acquainted with the spiritual practice of architecture there, as I did when I was at Milan Polytechnic.

Curiously enough, however, from a Feng Shui perspective, some of Frank Lloyd Wright's great masterpieces of architecture do not always appear to be the most comfortable structures to live in. Like many other masterpieces of architecture, some of his most original works have become museums or showcases, not happily inhabited residences. Here I found myself back to square one in my dilemma: is it the style, the design, or something else that makes a house a dream home?

In my search for a divine rule, I eventually became better acquainted with the Asian community and with the concept of a spiritual practice of architecture. I learned that Feng Shui, this Chinese secret so highly valued in Hong Kong, Taiwan, Singapore, and throughout Southeast Asia, deals with metaphysics and the study of what is going on in a building on an *energy* level that the eye cannot see. Of course, I am not talking about the effects of radioactive material or asbestos, but rather the patterns of the natural life-force energy as it flows into and through a building.

Yes, it is a secret because it cannot be seen, so one has to be sensitive enough to understand its dynamics and, also, one must study with a good teacher. This is how to truly learn, otherwise Feng Shui remains a secret.

When I finally began to learn this secret, I knew I had come to the end of my search and the beginning of my new apprenticeship as a junior traditional Feng Shui master under the tutelage of Master "Sifu" Lawrence Sang (*sifu* is a Cantonese term meaning a guide who imparts a tradition to an apprentice). From Master Sang, who was originally from Hong Kong, I learned the art and science of traditional Feng Shui, with the idea of integrating it with my architectural background. After many years of study, Master Sang came to refer to me as his "Italian daughter" (a great honor for a Westerner), and he also became very close with my parents.

I spent several years with my nose buried in notes from his teachings and, through the lens of this newfound information, I "read" the energy patterns of all sorts of buildings, such as residential, commercial, new, old, historical sites and celebrity homes, to see the practical effects of the theory on real life. I built my own archive of personal experiences and continued to be astounded at the close relationship between the information revealed in my readings and my clients' personal stories.

In some cases I was faced with very dramatic situations.

Such episodes touched me greatly. I wished I could have consulted on those buildings while they were still under construction, and therefore have been able to recommend changes that could have been easily implemented, and possibly change the building's energy effects on the inhabitants.

At the same time, my concepts about design were transformed dramatically. When I looked at a building before, I saw an assembly of walls, doors, and windows, while now I see patterns of energy, some favorable and some not, as well as the flow of life-force energy from room to room. Now, I decide on a layout or a design based on this "energy blueprint."

Of course, I do my best to recommend Feng Shui solutions that are also very functional and in good taste. I enjoy working with architects and designers who both understand that my goal is to make a space as comfortable and as energetically balanced as possible for the clients, and who will work with me toward this vision both from an aesthetic and a functional point of view. I am not attached to a particular design style; I leave that up to the owner and the architect. Whether the design is Modern, Tudor or Colonial, I still look at the energy blueprint of a building and its relationship to its occupants before recommending anything.

This book can act as a doorway to the metaphysical aspects of design and decorating by providing a new understanding of how life-force energy affects a home. These elements are important because they will eventually affect the occupants, who by the mere act of living there, will be in tune with the building's energy. Any unbalance present in the structure will be reflected in their lives. The secret in this case is to approach the subject with openness and with an adventurous spirit of experimentation. Whether you have read other books on similar topics or this is the first, you are likely to discover a rather different perspective.

Those who first read drafts of this manuscript reported an interest in applying the suggestions, as well as a willingness to know more. Some have pinpointed cases of friends and acquaintances living in buildings that they now recognize as having "bad Feng Shui." Most of them now acknowledge a desire to build, rent, or buy with the assistance or supervision of an expert.

If you like, you can read through this book once and then use it as a reference guide for home or office design and furnishing. If you are in the process of building or buying, you can use it as your checklist for the various aspects you might be considering. Many architects and designers who are introduced to Feng Shui principles subsequently discover a brand new awareness and perception of architecture and the constructed environment around them. If you are in the field of architecture, design, or construction, you can also consider this a formal study aid, digest the contents of each chapter, and then use the book in your daily work.

In order to help you better understand the practical application that constitutes most of the book, I have offered an initial overview of the history, the underlying theory, and the more abstract aspects of Feng Shui. These are contained in the first few chapters. If you'd rather focus on the direct application, you can skip the beginning of the book, go to Chapter Five, and perhaps read the historical and theoretical material later.

It is my wish that you enjoy this book and become more aware of what may be affecting your life in relation to the buildings where you live and work. Such perceptions are part of expanding consciousness and knowledge, which could supply a foundation for building greater awareness in this new century.

Simona F. Mainini, Dr. Arch.

A note about spelling variation: In general, I have attempted to use the Pin Yin translation system developed in China, with a few exceptions occurring where the Wade-Giles spelling variation is part of a published work or is much more widely accepted (such as with the use of *I Ching* rather than *Yi Jing*).

Chapter 1

WHAT, WHEN, HOW
AND WHY

There is one thing stronger than all the armies in the world,
and that is an idea whose time has come.

—Victor Hugo

What is Feng Shui?

Feng Shui is the ancient Chinese natural science of building design and placement. It is sometimes called Geomantic science, which is the discipline of understanding from the innate wisdom of the Earth how to live in harmony with it by properly siting, orienting, designing, and decorating the buildings where we live and work. That is why it is also known as the *art of placement* (of a building on the land).

The Wisdom of the Earth

It is interesting to compare the Asian view of the world with our Western counterpart. Often, we believe we are so tough that we can control everything and anything; that if we simply push forward we can achieve everything we want. We may be more or less fortunate, but most of us tend to chalk it up to chance with phrases like, "Yeah . . . can't control luck!" We also wish that once we get to where we want to be, we could freeze the moment, somehow guaranteeing that we do not lose all that we have created. As I am sure many will agree (even the most successful of us), constantly pushing our way to the top is tremendously time-energy-health-consuming and no matter how hard we try, change is always lurking around the corner especially when we least expect it.

The ancient Chinese vision is a bit different: To get the best from the effort we put into life, whether with work or family or preserving health, it is important to be aligned with the ongoing changes in order to see them coming, and to be able to adjust accordingly. Ancient Chinese masters believed that change is caused by transformational patterns of the life-force energy, or *Qi* (pronounced CHEE), on the planet.

Once you know how the life-force energy operates, you can make sure to be where the energy, or Qi (*ch'i*) of the Earth is more positive, more prosperous, and more supportive. Feng Shui was created especially for this purpose. Doing this will support you during these changes and increase the potential of favorable outcomes by allowing you to plan your life, while taking advantage of the support of the surrounding Qi.

Sometimes we may have to arrange our building interiors in a slightly different way than we might otherwise choose, or maybe even change the color of our walls and furniture. Other times we may have to plan the proper timing of a new construction or change the proposed orientation of our buildings or their interior layout. In all of these cases, the purpose is not to force us into doing something other than what we had planned, but rather to make us aware of a more effective way in which we could invest our time and money for the purpose of achieving the best possible results with the least effort. This is the core teaching: "going with the flow of the Qi energy" and using change to our advantage instead of resisting it stubbornly. How much easier can it be?

By observing the cycles of nature and consequently its energy transformations, Feng Shui can align us and our buildings with the energy of our planet. By being aware of how our environment affects us, we can learn how to transform our lives, feel more supported by the world around us, and ultimately achieve with ease and enthusiasm all that we set our minds on: health, happiness, love, fulfilling relationships, success, and prosperity.

In this Ching Dynasty illustration, a geomancer is using his compass (Lo Pan). The geomancer, or hsien-sheng, was the first and most prized consultant in the entire building design process. Even today, the Feng Shui analysis of a site precedes any other and is fundamental to the subsequent planning steps.

When Was It Created?

The roots of Traditional Feng Shui are very ancient, and its basic principles are the same as those of Traditional Chinese Medicine and acupuncture. As far back as 3000 B.C., the geomancer, or what we would now call a Feng Shui master, was responsible for selecting a building's site, orientation, and time of construction according to the energy patterns of the Earth. Traditionally, this person was the first to be consulted and the most prized architect or designer in the entire building process.

The Origins

Some archeological sites in China that indicate the use of Feng Shui-related concepts go as far back as 6,000 years. The first formal practices of an early form of divination may have appeared around 2800 B.C. in the time of the legendary founder of the Chinese culture, Fu Xi (also spelled Fu Hsi or Fu Shi). In addition to pioneering the development of writing and mathematics, as well as astronomical and environmental observation, this ancient sage determined the hidden essence of nature and divined a sequence of eight mathematical symbols (*ba-gua, or pa kua*), which represent the eight directions, essential elements, and basic energy frequencies that exist throughout the cosmos. Today, these mathematical symbols are expressed as *trigrams*, stacks of three lines each.

"... when Fu Hsi had come to the rule of all under heaven, looking up he contemplated the brilliant forms exhibited in the sky, and looking down he surveyed the patterns on the earth. He contemplated the ornamental appearances of birds and beasts and their differing suitability. Near at hand, in his own person, he found things for consideration; and at a distance, the same in things in general. Upon this he devised the Eight Trigrams to show fully the attributes of the spiritual intelligence operating secretly, and to classify the qualities of myriad things."

Ta Chuan (Great Treatise of the *I Ching*) - Section 2

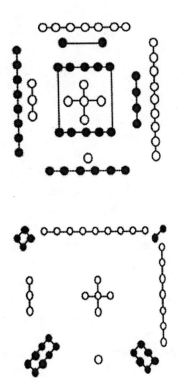

The He Tu (above) and Luo Shu (below)diagrams as they originally appeared on the backs of the legendary dragon-horse and turtle. The black
and white dots refer to the Yin and Yang polarities, while the number of
dots refers to the Trigram numbers. The Pre-Heaven and Post Heaven
orders of trigrams were later derived from these two diagrams.

He Tu

A Chinese legend relates the discovery of the trigrams as follows:
One day, while meditating along the River He (Yellow River), Fu
Xi saw a mythological "dragon-horse" rise from the water. The
horse had black and white spots on its back, representing numerical
relationships that were arranged in a specific order. This pattern
became the *He Tu* (River Chart or Diagram). Its configuration was

thought to represent an ideal state of perfection. These representations were later organized in a specific order, called the Pre-Heaven or Earlier Heaven (*Xian Tian*) Sequence. In the philosophy of the Tao, this order represents the intrinsic energies with which humans are endowed at and before birth.

The Sage Kings

Around 2300 B.C., China experienced the Great Flood, similar to the one described in the Bible at the time of Noah. This flood lasted for many years, much longer than the forty-day biblical deluge. During that period, there were three wise rulers, Yao, Shun, and Yu, who became known as the "Three Sage Kings." Yu succeeded in controlling the flooding, after which he became the founder of the first dynasty of China, the Xia (Hsia) Dynasty. Legend has it that one day, while meditating along the River Luo, Emperor Yu saw a giant turtle with a strange arrangement of markings carved on its shell, rising from the water. These markings could be expressed numerically and were later transcribed into a grid pattern of nine numbers known as the Luo Shu (Luo River Writing). This event occurred several hundred years after Fu Xi was said to have seen the spotted dragon-horse in the River He.

In the subsequent Shang period, the study of *Yin/Yang* principles (the principles of complementary opposites) and the Luo Shu gave rise to the Post-Heaven, Later Heaven, or After Heaven sequence of trigrams, the *Hou Tian Ba Gua* (eight trigrams of the later heaven). In the eleventh century B.C., the Eight Trigrams were rearranged into a new configuration of 64 hexagrams by King Wen Wang of the state of Zhou. These models expressed movement, interaction, and change.

During the Zhou Dynasty period, these early philosophical and mathematical ideas were known as the *Zhou Yi*. They were later collected and formalized, along with subsequent commentaries written over several centuries, to become the widely accepted version of the *I Ching* (sometimes spelled *Yi Jing*), known in English as the *Book of Changes* or *Change Classic*. Confucius, who was the last of the attributed authors of the commentaries known as the *Ten Wings*, described the interaction of the eight trigrams in the world:

> *"Thunder brings about movement, wind brings about dispersion, rain brings about moisture, the sun brings about warmth, the mountain brings about standstill, the lake brings about pleasure, the heaven brings about leadership, earth brings about shelter."*

Confucius, Ten Wings, Shuo Kua (Eight Wing)

Confucius saw the cosmic interplay of the universe's energies in the trigrams and described their unity in lyrical and seemingly paradoxical terms:

> *"Heaven and Earth determine the direction. The forces of mountain and lake are united. Thunder and wind arouse each other. Water and fire do not combat each other. Thus are the eight trigrams intermingled. Counting that which is going into the past depends on the forward movement. Knowing that which is to come depends on the backward movement. This is why the Book of Changes has backward numbers."*

Confucius, Ten Wings, Shuo Kua

Fundamental to the understanding of both Feng Shui and the *I Ching*, the Eight Trigrams are each composed of a series of three horizontal lines, some continuous (Yang) and some broken (Yin). In the *I Ching*, the trigrams are combined in sets of two to create hexagrams. The trigrams were derived from mathematical values and relationships. By interpreting these trigrams, the ancients saw that it was possible not only to live in harmony with the universe, but also to understand human destiny.

"In the ancient times the holy sages made the book of changes
. . . They contemplated the changes in the dark and the light
and established the hexagrams in accordance with them. They
brought about movements in the firm and the yielding, and
thus produced the individual lines. They put themselves in accord
with the universe and its power, and in conformity with this
laid down the order of what is right. By thinking through the
order of the outer world to the end, and by exploring the law of
their nature to the deepest core, they arrived at an understanding
of fate."

Confucius, *Ten Wings, Shuo Kua*

The He Tu and the Luo Shu writings were not only famous
and respected as legends, they also garnered credibility in arch-
aeological discovery. Since paper was not yet available in the days
of antiquity, it was common practice to use animal bones and
tortoise shells to record information. Tortoise shells were also
used as divination tools. The use of tortoise shell was so
predominant that one species became extinct.

At the end of the nineteenth century an incredible discovery
took place by accident. A "dragon-bone" (the skeletal fossil of a
prehistoric mammal) used in the prescriptive medications of a
Beijing herbal shop was discovered to have ancient Chinese
characters carved on it. The research of Professor Wang Kuo-
Wei deter-mined that the bone came from one of the most
ancient oracle-bone archives ever found. According to the
archeologists, not only did it belong to the King Diviners'
archive (Shang Dynasty), but the characters used were much
more ancient than any of those dating from the Bronze Age, a
time during which most scholars had previously thought writing
was first developed.

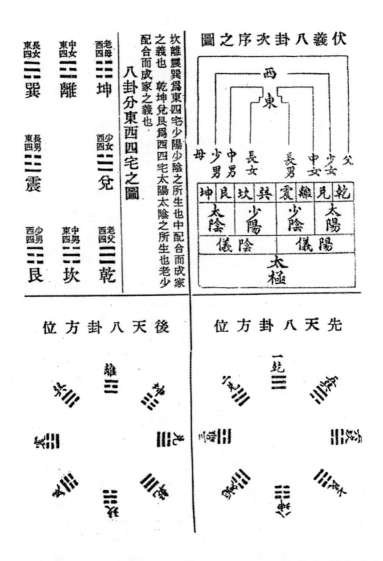

The Eight Trigrams as they derive from the Yin/Yang principle. At the bottom of the page, the trigrams are arranged according to the Post Heaven order (*Luo Shu*) on the left and the Pre-Heaven order (*He Tu*) on the right. This illustration is from *Master Shan's Xuan Kong Study* (*Shan Shi Xuan Kong Xue*) Tang Dynasty, 600-900 C.E.

Luo Shu

The Luo Shu sequence is also known as the "Inner-World Arrangement," and it works in conjunction with the He Tu. While the He Tu represents the ideal perfection of the heavenly order, the Luo Shu represents transformation and change through the relationship of human energy with that of the environment. The Luo Shu speaks of the balanced imperfection of our world and while the notion of balance in imperfection may appear contradictory, Confucius clarifies this paradox. He explains that the wheel of perpetual change ultimately elevates us to unity and perfection:

> *"Changes come forth in the sign of the Arousing; he brings all things to completion in the sign of the Gentle; he causes creatures to perceive one another in the sign of the Clinging (light); he causes them to serve one another in the sign of the Receptive. He gives them joy in the sign of the Joyous; he battles in the sign of the Creative; he toils in the sign of the Abysmal; he brings them to perfection in the sign of Keeping Still."*

> Confucius, *Ten Wings, Shuo Kua*

Kan Yu: Celestial Observations

Though Confucius and Lao Tzu contributed to the evolution of Feng Shui with their commentaries on the *I Ching*, back in those days this secret science was still mostly based on the Yin/Yang theory and it was known by an older name, *Kan Yu*, often interpreted as referring to heaven and earth or above and below. Even modern practitioners sometimes refer to the Feng Shui discipline as Kan Yu.

Kan Yu also entailed the observations of patterns in celestial bodies (Heaven Qi) and their effects on Earth (Earth Qi). Practitioners noticed how certain planetary patterns could bring about natural disasters, inclement weather, or bring sadness to people, while other patterns set the stage for a peaceful environment resulting in prosperity, harmony, and happiness. Little by little, these patterns were codified into cause-and-effect theories from which the formulas for their applications were derived. They were first formally applied during the Han Dynasty period, in about A.D. 200. Mention of the term *Feng Shui* first appeared in print in the *Zhang Shu*, or *Book of Burial*, around A.D. 300, and additional theories of the Feng Shui practice began to emerge during the Tang Dynasty (A.D. 618-960).

During this period of political stability, the arts, literature, and the sciences flourished. Astronomy, geography, surveying, and architecture each played a role in the development of Feng Shui, as well as the use of the *Lo Pan*, or *Luo Pan*, the geomancer's compass, an instrument whose earliest models date back to 100 B.C.; it consisted of a plate divided into ordinal and cardinal directions. The central compass utilized a spoon-shaped magnet, and the surrounding surface plate had information carved into it. Later versions contained movable rings with eight groups of three segments, or trigrams. Although the earlier Lo Pan looks very different from compasses used today, its essence and the information it conveyed are not very different.

How Was It Created?

Despite Feng Shui's development, emperors, nobles, and a privileged few others deliberately kept it secret to secure their power. All literature on Feng Shui was forbidden to the commoners.

To learn this ancient metaphysical art, a student would require a degree of education, which in those days was a rarity among the commoners who were mostly illiterate.

The secrets were learned through apprenticeship and often passed down through generations within families. Practitioners served the elite exclusively and were generously rewarded, while dissenters who attempted to practice outside the emperor's court risked their lives.

Detail of the ancient compass, in its original design, with the central needle resembling a spoon (Gene Ogami photography).

The Secret Science of Feng Shui

Toward the end of the Zhou Dynasty, about 200 B.C., China entered a dark period during which the emperor forbade his subjects to read and study. Books were destroyed or sequestered inside the emperor's palace, including those concerning Feng Shui principles. The only books left to the people were those on medicine, agriculture, and divination (*I Ching*). During this period, the various interpretations of the classic *Book of Changes* were re-edited into one official version. All other versions were then destroyed. Fortunately, around 1975 the discovery of the Mawangdui graves, dating back to 168 B.C., brought to light many unedited ancient books, including a few versions of the *I Ching* apparently preserved by a scholar in a region far from the emperor's influence.

Master Yang and Master Zeng

When the Tang Dynasty fell after a farmers' rebellion in the late ninth century A.D., a court official named Yang Yun-Song, fled the imperial palace with valuable and irreplaceable archival books of Feng Shui calculations written by a famous master mathematician called Chiu Yen-Han. Hidden in the mountains of his homeland in the Jiangxi (Chiang Sze) Province, not only did Yang pursue his studies, but he also applied Feng Shui to help the poor improve their lives. In those days, the term "poor" indicated anyone other then the emperor or the aristocrats belonging to the ruling class. Later, Master Yang became known as The Savior of the Poor.

Yang became the most highly respected Feng Shui scholar and spent most of his life developing the use of the geomancer compass and the Xuan Kong (Nine Palaces/mysterious void/time-space) system. Xuan Kong is a time-space theory of directional energy as it interacts with geological and architectural forms and is then applied to specific situations. This great master emphasized the role of virtue and compassion in the practice of Feng Shui, and he is still remembered today as the one who perfected and brought this long-held secret to the common folk. Most contemporary schools of Feng Shui trace their roots back to Master Yang and the Jiangxi School.

Despite Master Yang's egalitarianism, the dissemination of Feng Shui was still limited. Only male apprentices were selected, most from within a master's family, and only one master was chosen in each generation.

The first student of Master Yang was Master Zeng Wen-Shan, and Master Zeng later imparted Feng Shui training to his entire family. However, when one of master Zeng's daughters married, to her family's great disappointment, she taught her husband, Liao Yu, the secret science she had learned from her father.

When Liao's daughter married, she did the same and taught her husband, Lai Ren-Wen, what she had learned. To stop the flight of information outside the Zeng family, women were thereafter forbidden to learn Feng Shui.

41

Feng Shui Then and Now

Scholars of the Song Dynasty (960-1279), such as Shao Yung, made significant contributions to the study of the He Tu and the Luo Shu and demonstrated the mathematical qualities of the trigram arrangements. After China subsequently fell to the Mongols of the Yuan Dynasty, Feng Shui was suppressed along with most of the Chinese culture. During the Ming Dynasty (1368-1644), Feng Shui's development diminished, and it became a routine practice. During the latter part of this dynasty, books on Feng Shui multiplied and became available to the masses. Various writers had differing views, and they soon began to contend with one another. As a result, many people became self-proclaimed Feng Shui masters after reading a few texts. The practice of Feng Shui was often abused, and many practitioners took advantage of superstitious and illiterate people. However, a few genuine masters belonging to the oldest families continued to contribute to Feng Shui's development by focusing on the Lo Pan, understanding how people and locations interact together, and practicing proper timing.

The arrangement of the Eight Trigrams is organized according to the principals of binary mathematics. In the seventeenth century, the "discovery" of binary mathematics by German mathematician Gottfried von Liebnitz brought concepts of the *I Ching* into vogue in the Western world. In fact, Liebnitz had been introduced to the system by a missionary who returned to Europe after living in China.

When the People's Republic of China was created in 1949, traditional Chinese cultural practices including Feng Shui were banned. Feng Shui went underground in China and was only practiced openly in Hong Kong, Taiwan, and some other parts of Southeast Asia.

Today, the growing interest in Feng Shui in the United States, Canada, Australia, and Europe is partly attributable to Asian immigration particularly from Hong Kong and Taiwan. In spite of its increasing popularity, Feng Shui is sometimes misinterpreted. Ornaments such as mirrors, crystals, and wind chimes, more folklorist remedy than genuine Feng Shui practice, often hang on the walls and doors of Chinese homes and have become a fashionable trend amongst Westerners as well.

Due to its increasing popularity, some consultants learn a few rudiments of the Feng Shui theory and then mix them with symbolism and superstition, which can lead the practice of Feng Shui at times to be associated with religion. It is important to remember that those with true knowledge have always carefully guarded this discipline and that those with a superficial understanding often misinterpret it. The teachings of a well-respected teacher are the key to unlocking the secrets of this great and ancient science and it is the only method for its proper dissemination.

Why Was It Created?

The study of the trigrams and subsequent diagrams engaged sages, wise man, scholars and kings, for many centuries. It is difficult to say how reliable the legends are, for example were these ancient symbols really imprinted on the backs of a dragon-horse and a water turtle, and if so, were they living animals, or rather ancient materials used to store information (horsehide parchment and tortoise shell) prior to the invention of paper?

In more contemporary times, some researchers have speculated that this information may actually be all that is left of a previous, very advanced civilization, perhaps Atlantis or a similar culture. Others have gone so far as to wonder if they were gifts from an alien civilization.

The information used in Feng Shui includes a solar calendar, a directional system based on Magnetic North, and the cycle of seasons peculiar to our planet. The cycle of seasons is determined by the inclination of the Earth rotating on its axis, along with its orbit and period of revolution around the sun. These criteria, which are basic to Feng Shui formulas and principles, are qualities unique to Planet Earth.

It appears clear that the Eight Trigrams contain astounding information which sages and kings labored to unveil and succeeded in doing so. The continuous and broken lines of the trigrams form the basic tools of the Yin/Yang theory, as well as the Five Elements theory. It is a combination of the Eight Trigrams that gave rise to the 64 hexagrams of the *I Ching* and all the disciplines that were created as a consequence, not to mention the formulation of modern binary mathematics that took place only a few hundred years ago, a system already contained in trigrams discovered several thousand years earlier.

The *I Ching* is, to this day, considered both the book of all wisdom and a light in the darkness by Chinese scholars concerned with mathematics, traditional medicine, astronomy, philosophy, and geomancy. The fact that the trigrams were discovered rather then formulated puts us, particularly Westerners, face to face with a mystery of the magnitude of the Sphinx, the Pyramids or Stonehenge.

The Map of the Creator

In support of the hypothesis of a superior ancient civilization, I included the following article translated in English by Vera Solovieva and published in the Russian newspaper *Pravda* on April 30, 2002:

THE MAP OF "THE CREATOR"

A find by Bashkir scientists contrary to traditional notions of human history: [a] stone slab which is 120 million years [old] covered with the relief map of Ural Region.

This seems to be impossible. Scientists of Bashkir State University have found indisputable proofs of an ancient highly developed civilization's existence. The question is about a great plate found in 1999, with a picture of the region done according to an unknown technology. This is a real relief map. Today's military has almost similar maps. The map contains civil engineering works: a system of channels with a length of about 12,000 km, weirs, and powerful dams. Not far from the channels, diamond-shaped grounds are shown, whose destination is unknown. The map also contains some inscriptions. . . . At first, the scientists thought that it was Old Chinese language. Though, it turned out that the inscriptions were done in a hieroglyphic-syllabic language of unknown origin. The scientists never managed to read it . . . .

"The more I learn the more I understand that I know nothing," admits Alexander Chuvyrov, doctor of physical and mathematical science and a professor at Bashkir State University. Namely, Chuvyrov made the sensational find. In 1995, the professor and his post-graduate student from China, Huan Hun, decided to study the hypothesis of the possible migration of an Old Chinese population to the territory of Siberia and Ural. In an expedition to Bashkiria, they found several rock carvings done in Old Chinese language. These finds confirmed the hypothesis of Chinese migrants. The inscriptions were read. They mostly contained information about trade bargains, marriage and death registration.

Though, during the searches, notes dated the eighteenth century were found in archives of the Ufa governor-general. They reported about 200 unusual stone slabs which were situated not far from the Chandar village in the Nurimanov region. Chuvyrov and his colleague at once decided that slabs could be connected with Chinese migrants.

Work was launched in Chandar. After having dug out the slab, the searchers were [struck] by its size: it was 148 cm high (59 inches), 106 cm wide (42 inches) and 16 cm thick (6 inches). While it weighed at least one ton . . . the scientists could not [trust] their eyes . . . "At first sight," Chuvyrov says, "I understood that was not a simple stone piece, but a real map, and not a simple map, but a three-dimensional one. You can see it yourself.

" . . . The group of Russian and Chinese specialists in the field of cartography, physics, mathematics, geology, chemistry, and Old Chinese language, discovered that the slab contains the map of the Ural region, with the rivers Belya, Ufimka, Sutolka," Alexander Chuvyrov said, while showing the lines on the stone to the journalists. "You can see the Ufa Canyon—the break of the earth's crust, stretched out from the city of Ufa to the city of Sterlitimak. At the moment, Urshak River runs over the former canyon." The map is done on a scale 1:1.1 km.

[The] geological structure of the slab was determined: it consists of three levels. The base is 14 cm thick (5 inches), made of the firmest

dolomite. The second level is probably the most interesting, "made" of diopside glass. The technology of its treatment is not known to modern science. Actually, the picture is marked on this level. While the third level is 2 mm thick (3/16 of an inch) and made of calcium porcelain protecting the map from external impact.

"It should be [noted]," the professor said, "that the relief has not been manually made by an ancient stonecutter. It is simply impossible. It is obvious that the stone was machined." X-ray photographs confirmed that the slab was of artificial origin and had been made using precision tools.

At first, the scientists supposed that the ancient map could have been made by the ancient Chinese, because of vertical inscriptions on the map. As well known, vertical literature was used in the Old Chinese language before the third century . . . . After the meeting with his colleagues from Hunan University, he completely gave up the . . . "Chinese track." The scientist concluded that the porcelain covering the slab had never been used in China . . . . Chuvyrov, however, stated that he deciphered one sign on the map: it signifies the latitude of today's city of Ufa.

The longer the slab was studied, the more mysteries appeared. On the map, a giant [irrigation] system could be seen: in addition to the rivers, there are two 500-meter-wide channel systems, 12 dams, 300-500 meters wide, approximately 10 km long and 3 km deep each. The dams most likely helped in turning water to either side, while to create them over one quadrillion cubic meters of earth was shifted . . . . As a physicist, Alexander Chuvyrov supposes that now mankind can build only a small part of what is pictured on the map. According to the map, initially, the Belaya River had an artificial [riverbed].

It was difficult to determine even an approximate age for the slab. At first, [radiocarbon] analysis was carried out, and afterwards levels of the slab were scanned with a uranium chronometer, although the investigations showed different results and the age of the slab remained unclear. While examining the stone, two shells were found on its surface. The age of one of them . . . is about 500 million years, and of the second one . . . about 120 million years . . . . "The map was probably created at the time when the Earth's magnetic pole was situated in the today's area of Franz Josef Land. This was exactly 120 million years ago," professor Chuvyrov says.

What could be the destination of the map? That is probably the most interesting thing. Materials of the Bashkir find were already investigated in Center of Historical Cartography in Wisconsin, USA. The Americans were amazed. According to them, such three-dimensional map could have only one destination—a navigational one, while it could be worked out only through aerospace survey . . . . The technology of compiling such maps demands super-power computers and aerospace survey from the Shuttle. So, who created this map? Chuvyrov, while speaking about the unknown cartographers, is wary: "I do not like to talk about some UFO or extraterrestrial. Let us call the author of the map simply—the creator."

Now, the scientists are sure that the map is only a fragment of a big map of the Earth.

In the meantime, Bashkir scientists sent out information about their find to different scientific centers around the world, and in several international congresses they have already given reports on the subject: The Civil Engineering Works Map of an Unknown Civilization of South Ural."

The find of Bashkir scientists has no analogues.

Translated by Vera Solovieva

Chapter	HOW FENG SHUI AND
2	**ARCHITECTURE** **WORK TOGETHER**

What Feng Shui Can and Cannot Do

Many pages have been written about the wonderful achievements of Feng Shui. Based on universal laws observable in nature, Feng Shui can be used as a tool for growth . . . and like any tool, it must be used properly. Therefore, to avoid misinterpretation and to save us from unrealistic expectations, it is important to understand what Feng Shui can and cannot do.

- **Feng Shui can create a healthier environment and thus advance our well-being.** By improving our living space, it can create a *preventively* healthier environment, it can increase our mental alertness in business and finance, and therefore also foster our prosperity, but it cannot cure cancer or create wealth on its own.

- **Feng Shui can assist us in selecting a prosperous location for a house or business.** Feng Shui cannot bring us million-dollar deals if we are not working toward them. In other words, we should not expect financial success if we are at home watching TV instead of creating opportunity for ourselves.

- Feng Shui can make our life's journey clearer, but it can neither change our destiny nor help us to avoid change in our life.

Change is a part of life, and sometimes we have to make difficult decisions. Feng Shui is a tool that can help us make those decisions. By forecasting cyclical changes, Feng Shui helps us maximize the positive effects of those changes and minimize the negative.

- **Designing a space with Feng Shui places us in better harmony with the environment and all the elements of nature.** By making our environment work to maximize and use the potential of our space, Feng Shui can ensure that harmonious life-force energy enters at all times. This alone can enhance our opportunity and destiny. However, it cannot guarantee that we will win the lottery or that Mr. or Mrs. Right will knock at our door if we never buy the ticket or leave the house to meet new people.

Feng Shui, Destiny, and Luck

Consulting for people both in the U.S. and abroad, I have found that every standing building is subject to the energy of its environment. In fact, whether a building is planned to follow Feng Shui principles or not, Qi (life-force energy) still flows around it, and time and orientation will definitely play a role in the nature of the building's energy. The building will have a specific Feng Shui character, whether good or bad. Making an evaluation of an existing building typically means making the owners aware of the existing conditions and giving them recommendations on how to correct imbalances and disharmony in terms of the way the Qi flows in various areas. In the vast majority of cases, a building that was originally built with poor Feng Shui elements will unfavorably affect the lives of all of its occupants over the years.

I evaluated a house in Southern California's San Fernando Valley a few years ago that appeared to have a long list of Feng Shui "no-nos." The client had contacted me because of financial difficulties he had encountered over the few years they had lived in the house.

As I learned during our session, his wife also experienced several health problems that developed after they moved into the house.

I asked them if they knew anything about the previous owners. To my surprise, they were very well aware of an ongoing situation. In the short life of this building, there had been four different occupants. The previous owners had either lost all their money or their jobs and had to sell in foreclosure, had divorced and had sold the house as a consequence, or had passed away under dramatic circumstances!

It is not unusual to hear about buildings such as this one (the word building will be used interchangeably with the word house throughout the book), and it is helpful to be aware of this background information when purchasing an existing building. In Feng Shui terms, history often repeats itself. With few exceptions, when a building has "negative energy" it affects all the people living there throughout its history. This is not necessarily because previous owners leave bad energy when they depart, but rather because when the potential for the building is not very positive it affects each of its occupants one after the other.

It is always a big red flag for me when a client reports certain negative background information about a building that has just been purchased or is about to be purchased. Comments may be similar to the following examples:

"This is so great – this building is worth three times the price, but the owner just went bankrupt and has to sell."

"The building is in foreclosure; it is such a great deal!"

" . . . It's been empty for several years . . . ."

"One of the owners passed away shortly after they bought it . . . ."

"The owners divorced. One kept the house and got married again and then divorced again! Can you believe it?"

Yes, I can believe it, and I also believe that destiny is destiny. Perhaps those people were meant to live in those buildings and to experience life the way they did. However, I also believe that when you decide to have a good Feng Shui consultant look at a property

FENG SHUI FOR ARCHITECTURE

for you, it means that you are being lead to a better destiny because the Feng Shui consultant can advise you against a potentially unfortunate house.

Not everyone requests the help of a Feng Shui consultant; perhaps they just decide to live out their destiny blindly. Those who do and who accept the advice usually have a favorable experience.

I've also noticed that, in their search for the perfect house, clients will sometimes encounter several different yet all unfavorable Feng Shui houses. Although enticed by the deal and by the convenience of the place, they may take my advice and look into a different opportunity. Then a month or two, or even a year later, they will happen to find a cluster of very favorable Feng Shui houses, all very nice, all very pretty, all "just right" for them. This is an example of a change of fortune in their lives. They were destined to live in a good house, but the right time had not come yet, so all the houses they found initially were really not good for them. It's not until the "heaven's Qi" effects on their "personal Qi" change that they enter a "lucky" time during which opportunities finally open up and good circumstances present themselves. Had they settled for an "unfavorable" house because they didn't have the patience to wait for a good one, things would have gone differently.

In the ancient Chinese culture, people knew that there was no point in rushing things only to tackle obstacle after obstacle. They knew that change is the engine of life, but they also learned to plan and wait patiently for the right time to take action. In our doing so, the outcome of change can be positive and enriching to our lives.

The Request for Feng Shui in Architecture

In the past, the teachings of Feng Shui were strictly reserved for scholars and sages. Currently we are experiencing a blending of disciplines, ethnicity, and trends, and it appears that Feng Shui is destined to become a "must know" for architects and those in the design fields. Professionals are finding that more and more often both Asian and non-Asian clients are requesting that these principles and techniques be applied to their buildings for the sake of their well-being as much as for their financial prosperity.

Although some may think of traditional Feng Shui as strictly associated with Chinese or Asian architecture—with pagoda roofs, red lacquer and golden trim—I have come to find that these principles can easily be applied to every design style. In fact, Feng Shui has nothing to do with style, per se. Designing a house using Feng Shui principles doesn't mean turning it into a Zen temple or a Chinese restaurant!

The rules of Feng Shui are related to the harmonious flow of the life force in our environment. This life force is present whether we are building in faux Beaux-arts or using a Modern style. While some styles may be more "Feng Shui friendly" than others in their design, the Feng Shui analysis will be comparable to ensure that a proper flow of the life-force energy is maintained throughout the building. *

I particularly advise using Feng Shui at the early planning stages of a building. After years of experience of working on existing buildings, I have sorted out situations that have more favorable effects, as well as situations that are less desirable. Planning from scratch offers me the possibility of creating the best possible Feng Shui on paper and then modeling the building around it. The earlier a plan is evaluated, the better. However, projects that are almost completed can, with some changes, also be transformed into excellent buildings that adhere to Feng Shui principles. This is certainly more effective and less expensive than altering a building after its completion.

For example, let's say one or two walls need to be moved. On paper, this can be drafted in a couple of hours, while in an existing building it may take a couple of weeks to achieve, with all the consequences and discomfort, dirt, and extra costs involved. I recommend the former process!

Steps in the Architectural Application of Feng Shui

In the design process, I have observed at least five different phases that may require the application of Feng Shui theories and principles. These will be reviewed in subsequent chapters covering the following topics:

1) Selecting the Site

Whether in the country or in the city, the surrounding property (and urban neighborhood) around our structure determines the flow and quality of the life force it receives. The effects may extend from the immediate surrounding area to a radius of several miles. We will apply exterior environmental guidelines to find a suitable place to locate our building. These are particularly important when looking for the right plot of land.

What if you already have a plot? If it is a good one, then that's great, you will have nothing to worry about! If not, we can learn how to correct it as much as possible to prevent any unfavorable effects. Landscape designers will also find these guidelines very helpful as they incorporate Feng Shui site corrections into their natural design. We will also learn how to avoid negative Qi, or Sha Qi, in the environment.

2) Designing the Interiors

We will learn design guidelines regarding how "visible Qi" flows inside a building. There are many effective ways to avoid energy dissipation with creative effective design features that can retain the precious life-force energy within the rooms. This section also briefly covers room-by-room dos and don'ts.

3) The Building's Energy

Together with building orientation, time and universal energy cycles form the core of analyzing the "invisible Qi" and they allow us to define the DNA of a building's energy. Time guidelines thus give rise to many energy combinations, making every house an individual case. Many contemporary Feng Shui practitioners do not apply these formulas because of their complexity and the level of experience required to fully understand them. Nevertheless, their accuracy is extraordinary. While points one and two are covered extensively in this book, these subsequent stages are very complex and remain the domain of a master.

4) Customizing the Building

By understanding "personal Qi" and its interaction with the building and making sure it is in harmony with the surrounding environment, we can improve our sense of comfort and well—being. Customizing a building involves matching people to buildings, favorable color and material use, and proper compass directions for the alignment of entrances, bedrooms, and other rooms of a house.

5) Construction Timing

Based on the occupants' dates of birth and the building orientation, it is possible to select the most auspicious time to start the construction of a building so that the "heavenly Qi" will support it, as well as its occupants, throughout its existence.

Selecting a Skilled Feng Shui Expert

Since the spaces we inhabit have a tremendous impact on the way we feel and walk through life, I advise anyone starting a project to design a building correctly from the start. Of course, as a Feng Shui expert, I recommend that people use the best traditional Feng Shui consultant available in their area. Even if clients have to bring in Feng Shui consultants from other cities, their skills are certainly worth the expense. As a medical patient, would you hire a dentist for an open-heart surgery because he or she lives in the same city as you, or would you rather take on the extra expense to travel to see specialists or bring them to you?

While ten or so years ago it was extremely hard to find a good traditional Feng Shui expert in the U.S. or Europe (they generally had to be flown in from Hong Kong or Taiwan), nowadays it is much easier to find them. Of course, not everyone is equal, and clients will do well to interview prospective consultants personally. In addition, ethnicity is no longer a sufficient characteristic to discern an expert.

We can easily assume, especially in the West, that because a consultant was born in China, Hong Kong, Singapore or Taiwan, he or she must be an expert; but this is not a reliable guideline. In fact, there are several Americans and Europeans who have achieved great expertise by studying with a master; on the other hand, no matter how hard they have tried, some Asian practitioners do not seem able to get beyond the beginner level. In other words, being Asian is not a criterion for Feng Shui expertise.

An expert consultant should have at least the following four points of criteria:

- The consultant will have studied continuously with a respected Feng Shui master—or with the longtime apprentice of an acknowledged master—for at least five years. Wandering students may look good on paper because they may appear to have seen it all and to know it all, but no respectable Feng Shui master would give away his precious knowledge to a drop-in-for-the-day inquirer. It is only with time and through dedication to learning that a teacher will know a student is seriously interested in acquiring knowledge and will voluntarily share advanced information and insight.

- Particularly, one should be cautious when choosing a "Certified Feng Shui Master". Few organizations offer this kind of certification after a crash course of only few weekends, at times by correspondence. It is doubtful that such condensed classes can prepare anyone to be a master, much less to certify one. Believing a master is created after a few short weeks discredits the 5000-year-old tradition of Feng Shui and does not honor the student or the client.

Collection of geomantic compasses, or Lo Pan. In the center is a replica of the ancient compass (Gene Ogami photography).

- The consultant will have built a background of experience for him/herself with a good range of clients. The only way to really know how the principals work is to see them in practice firsthand. In this way the consultant can become aware of various implications and build a solid archive to pass along to the next generation of Feng Shui practitioners to ensure that the information will remain intact.

- The consultant will be well versed in all aspects of traditional Feng Shui, and in particular the so-called Form and Compass schools. This shouldn't be a matter of favoring one over the other but rather the ability to use both since, as you are learning here, they are parts of the same complete body of knowledge. Needless to say, the consultant should be able to use a traditional Feng Shui compass (Lo Pan), as well as observing and detailing the pattern of Qi inside and outside a building. Using a Lo Pan is a qualifying criterion for expertise; be doubtful if an alleged expert does not use one.

New Buildings: the Feng Shui Architect

While a good Feng Shui expert can go a long way to rectify an existing building, I highly recommend finding a traditional Feng Shui expert who also has a background in architectural planning when designing a new commercial or residential building. The same recommendation applies if you are planning a major structural remodeling or renovation.

In my experience, it is crucial that your Feng Shui expert be able to relate to the architect, builder, developer, and engineer by having a good idea of what is involved in the conceptual design and creative process. Going back to our previous example: Would you hire an internist to perform open-heart surgery? However skilled such a physician might be, he or she doesn't practice the surgical specialization you require; and even with the best intentions, the skills may not be the ones you need.

I have many times witnessed beautiful building designs that were literally butchered by poor Feng Shui corrections, simply because the Feng Shui expert wasn't aware of the global vision of the project and could not relate his or her suggestions to the architect in a comprehensible manner. I have also witnessed architects completely alienated by supposed Feng Shui experts who made unreasonable requests, while having little to offer regarding the Feng Shui practice, and had no idea how illogical their requests truly were.

Such situations always make me very sad. Poor communication skills, poor understanding of the overall project, and low levels of expertise can often turn the typically joyful experience of the Feng Shui design of a brand new project into a nightmare and can potentially compromise or undermine the results.

As a cautionary note, I need to mention that I have also become aware of some architects or designers passing themselves off as Feng Shui connoisseurs. Upon inquiring about their background, I found out that they had read one or two garden-variety Feng Shui books and were now marketing their services as expert Feng Shui architects. Again, please remember that it is very important to do your homework when selecting a Feng Shui expert.

Western Adaptation

In the past ten years I have witnessed a proliferation of "Western schools" of Feng Shui. Many of these are, in fact, adaptations based on rather simplistic information, religious symbolism, and New Age-related concepts. Some of these "schools" claim either that Feng Shui is designed only for Asian people or that Westerners are not subject to the same Feng Shui principles as Asians. Many of these so-called schools primarily promote superstitious beliefs.

For example, the water element is very positive in Feng Shui; in an Asian residence, the occupants may supply it by way of a "lucky" koi pond in the garden, while in Western cultures this element might be transformed into a more acceptable "fish pond." However, a swimming pool may be equally as effective and even more greatly appreciated. An expert of Traditional Feng Shui will be aware that the water element is important, not the fish.

In some cases, I have seen other disciplines, from various "shaman traditions" to "space clearing" to "crystal therapy" to "building biology," advertised as Feng Shui. I am not sure why so many consultants and authors have arbitrarily decided to bury their disciplines under the Feng Shui blanket. Some of these methodologies are perfectly legitimate, and many are quiet interesting, and I believe they should be proudly advertised as what they really are, rather then confusing readers by teaching them concepts that have little or nothing to do with Feng Shui.

While I personally respect everyone's ethical choice in pursuing what they feel is right for them, I feel most comfortable studying, teaching, and practicing Traditional Feng Shui. This method carefully observes nature and the seasonal cycle of our planet and it has universal rules that can be applied to any location in the world and by people of any ethnicity. Its effectiveness is based more so on objective and scientific information than on belief systems.

Another common misconception is that Feng Shui is based on intuition. While I do believe strongly in the intuitive response that comes after having gathered knowledge and practice, I wouldn't hire a self-proclaimed "intuitive Feng Shui expert" to work for me.

Although it can be said that after acquiring a certain level of knowledge one may intuitively apply it based on experience, just as with any other profession that requires experience and skills, intuition per se is not enough. To quote a very skilled Australian colleague, "Feng Shui is not an intuition-based practice; it is a knowledge-based practice."

How would you like to be lying in a dentist's chair and be informed that the doctor didn't have any formal medical training but were told not to worry? "He is very intuitive and will be able to figure out what to do with your teeth!" or "He just took a weekend workshop with the best dentist in the country and now knows it all!"

Intuitive Designers and Professional Cooperation

After reading the latest Feng Shui book, some designers conclude that Feng Shui is really just a matter of intuition, and that good designers know these things instinctively anyway. As much as I would like to validate this point of view, I have to say that it is not quiet accurate. Yes, I have worked with some very wonderful designers and architects in my life whose taste and style I have truly admired. However, intuition only goes so far in relation to Feng Shui.

Some very original designs that I admired in the past actually gleaned a rather low score on the Feng Shui scale. Originality is valued in the arts, but when it comes to living in a building day after day, year after year, art may get old very fast if doesn't have something substantial behind it to back it up. Have you ever heard of a beautiful masterpiece of architecture whose owners lived a life of misery or moved out after two or three years to live in a more "low-key, regular, simple" house?

This is not a crusade against forward-thinking designers' houses. I love interesting design, and I used to favor the more original and push the envelope in my years as an architectural designer. I simply recommend that you check all the Feng Shui bases very carefully because there may be ways to counteract some inauspicious design features when using unique design. I have also seen some "designer buildings" that happened to be oriented in a favorable direction so that the energy was strong and healthy enough to support their special designs, although the designs themselves were not necessarily the best in terms of Feng Shui.

Interestingly enough, I have never heard any unfavorable comments from designers that I really respect and that I believe have been intuitively accurate in Feng Shui terms. The breed of architects and designers that are intuitively accurate tend to love their profession and are genuinely interested in giving their clients a hundred-percent effort. They also listen very carefully to feedback and analysis and ask as many questions as necessary to fully understand the Feng Shui boundaries with which they are working. The working process is also much easier for everyone.

Such designers are both very talented and very naturally intuitive. Not only that, they absorb the information offered and capitalize on it with their next projects. For my part, I do my best to provide them with Feng Shui guidelines without interfering with their creative processes. I attempt to let them express their talents freely, and I am very pleased to have worked with such creative people because I can see the beauty and the high quality in the final results of the projects.

When a client asks a designer to work with a Feng Shui expert, most professionals who respect their clients' requests will do their best to accommodate this, just as they would a request for a geologist and a civil or structural engineer. As are most other professionals, the Feng Shui consultant is hired by the client to apply his or her expertise to the best outcome of the project.

I always suggest that clients discuss this aspect with selected architects, builders, and contractors before hiring them. There is no point in forcing such concepts on them. In the end, it is perfectly legitimate if they do not feel comfortable with incorporating Feng Shui when a client requests them to do so. The client is then free to find another architect, builder, or contractor who can accommodate their request. I personally prefer to work as part of a professional team that is respectful of my input as much as I am of theirs, in order to make the design and building process easier for everyone and the results more aesthetically compelling.

Chapter 3

UNDERSTANDING LIFE-FORCE ENERGY

To properly understand Feng Shui theories and its applications in the design process, we must be able to grasp the inner dynamics of such work. Feng Shui is not just a series of instructions that can be followed verbatim to create some sort of magical incantation which, like the genie in the lamp, will then serve up the necessary results on a silver platter. Although some practitioners support such simplistic magical thinking, I have found that it doesn't quiet work that way.

Personally, I feel it is much more intriguing to discover and absorb the theory and the principles behind Feng Shui. These are fascinating, and by understanding them, you can actually find out for yourself how to resolve any exceptions to the rules that may not be included in this book.

Qi: The Raw Material of the Universe

The first step is to realize that the human body, as well as everything else around us, is not just made of physical matter but of energy as well. This energy interacts with its surroundings constantly, every moment of the day.

Practice pausing for a moment: close your eyes, feel the energy running through your body, and "see" all the energy around you with your imagination, you will eventually come to have a sense of the absolute interconnection between everything that exists. You need not try hard to be at one with it all, you already are!

In the *I Ching*, or *Book of Changes*, the universe is described as a continuous cyclical process of transformation. The *I Ching* propounds that if we understand these transformations as they relate to our surroundings, we can learn to live in harmony with our environment and achieve happiness and well being.

In particular, the energy of our homes, our offices, or any place where we spend a prolonged amount of time, interacts with the energy of our bodies to affect all the other related aspects of our lives, such as health, love lives and relationships, work performance, financial prosperity, and overall success. This energy runs through our bodies, and our bodies interact with it at all times, whether we are conscious of it or not.

The "energy" I am referring to is the *life-force energy* or *Qi.* This energy has a dynamic component that follows information input. In other words, it is not simply energy but it is energy with a function, or a scope, that is inherent in its nature.

For example, in Traditional Chinese Medicine, there are different levels of Qi, or specific life-force energies that feed the body. Each of these levels has a different function: the one that protects the cells is different from the one that makes the heart beat, which in turn is different from the one that makes the blood flow. Similarly, there are different types of Qi within a building that can have specific effects on people and their lives: some may prompt them to be argumentative, whereas other types may support creative talents or encourage romantic relationships or even enhance their physical fertility allowing them to create new life.

Ultimately, any and all of these manifestations (favorable or not) are actually coming from within us; whether we exhibit insecurity or aggressiveness, kindness or heartlessness, we can't create anything in our lives that we do not already possess hidden within ourselves. The energy of the building will simply "push the button," and the effect will manifest physically.

The aim of Feng Shui is to bring out the best hidden potential in each of us (whether that might result in good health or in making a million dollars) by harmonizing the flow of energy in our buildings.

Qi in the Ancient World

These days, Western culture tends to overanalyze and tear apart almost everything. As a result, we view physics, astronomy, medicine, philosophy, and religion as separate and distinct disciplines. In ancient China, however, these studies were all seen as unified and as sharing the same root. The art of living described in the *I Ching* united spiritual teachings, or metaphysics, and science, including medicine, chemistry, astronomy, astrology, geology, meteorology, seismology, and mathematics. This philosophy of wholeness resulted in the invention of the compass and the calendar, a process for the siting of graveyards, a system of agricultural timing, and last but not least, a complete set of guidelines for siting and building structures in harmony with the natural flow of energy in the environment: the art and science of Feng Shui.

In the natural environment, Qi is responsible for land formations such as mountains, the hues and shapes of leaves, soil productivity, crop fertility, the paths of streams, the color of the sky, the shapes of clouds, and even the constitution of people. In ancient Chinese astrology, Qi's all-pervasive quality in the environment was seen as the primary influence of the formation of the human personality. For example, someone born close to the mountains on a given year, month, day, and hour would be more prone to develop a kind and compassionate nature, while a person born close to a river or sea at the same time would tend to be more adaptive, agile, and sharp.

The key determinant at work is the life-force energy, which the ancients saw as the unifying principle in a world ultimately grounded in unity. By ensuring a proper flow of Qi in the environment (through Feng Shui), as well as in the body (through

Tai Qi, Qi Gong, therapeutic massage, and acupuncture), the ancients believed that a person's well-being could be preserved, that life could be prolonged and illnesses prevented, consequently having a favorable ripple effect on every aspect of theirs lives.

Qi and the Human Body

Good Qi circulation nurtures the internal organs and is as important as blood and other fluids in maintaining the body's health and vitality. According to Dr. Shen Zijin and Dr. Chen Zelin, authors of *Basis of Traditional Chinese Medicine*, "Qi is dynamic, active and invisible. It activates and warms the body and is thus ascribed to the Yang category. Blood, in Traditional Chinese Medicine terminology, is not very different from its understanding in Western Medicine. Both blood and body fluids have nourishing and moistening functions. Thus they belong to the Yin category. The natural history of a disease and the development of the human body from birth to death are closely affected by flows and changes of Qi, blood and body fluid."

Qi can produce and control the blood, warm and nourish the tissues, and build up resistance against disease, as well as activate the physiological functions of the internal organs. There are more than two dozen different types of Qi in the human body. Each of them has a specific function and is named differently according to the role it plays and the organs it serves.

Qi also commands the circulation of blood. It not only creates blood circulation but also helps to recycle the blood through its breakdown and regeneration. If the flow of Qi is interfered with, then the blood will stagnate and discomfort and fleeting pain may take place in the affected areas. Massive bleeding results from exhaustion of the Qi that holds the blood vessel together (Shen Ziyin and Chen Zelin, *The Basis of Traditional Chinese Medicine*, Shambala).

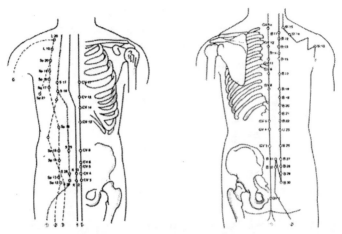

The life-force energy can be charted inside the human body through acupuncture meridians and channels. (Shen Ziyin and Chen Zelin, *The Basis of Traditional Chinese Medicine*, Shambala)

Qi and Other Cultures

The "Art of Living" theory was developed based on the concept that everything in nature follows energy patterns. Although the discipline of Feng Shui with its many branches and applications is unique to the Chinese culture, it was successively adopted by other Asian countries, as was the concept of life-force energy.

In China, the life-force is referred to as Qi (also spelled *ch'i*), while in Japan, Korea, and Polynesia it is known as *ki*. In India, the Hindus call it *prana* or *prana shakti*. Jewish mystics refer to it as *ruach*, the "breath of life" given by God to Adam and Eve at the moment of creation. In fact, *ruach* in Hebrew also means *wind*, an intriguing parallel to Feng Shui, since *wind* translates in Chinese as *feng*, one of the two primary elements of Feng Shui. The other critical element, *shui* or *water*, is also held by Jewish mystics to be a purifying force that removes negativity and reestablishes health and harmony.

There are intriguingly similar concepts throughout many of

the world's indigenous cultures. For example, in various American Indian spiritual practices, wind and water are essential spiritual elements. The Lakota people speak of *taku skan skan*, loosely translated as "something (sacred) moving," which implies the movement of spiritual energy and the power that animates all things. The phrase is also used to refer to the movement of the four winds. Water holds a very significant place in many American Indian traditions.

Qi and Modern Physics

In this century, the discovery of quantum physics has validated the ancient idea of global energetic connections between all elements of the physical world. Many analogies abound between the ancients' understanding of Qi and modern science. For example, physicists use the terms *strong forces* and *weak forces* to identify the energy that holds together electrons, protons, and neutrons and allows us to see them as physical matter. Though it may seem that these forces are inconsequential because an atom is microscopic in size, science demonstrates that they are indeed phenomenally powerful: splitting uranium atoms, for example, causes an atomic explosion. Thus what is invisible to the five senses ultimately contains within itself awesome physical power.

Gravity and electromagnetism are also part of the ways through which Qi manifests itself in nature. Ocean tides, weather patterns, and the pull of the Earth itself to keep all objects in place are some of the most fundamental processes in which the Earth Qi of gravitation affects our lives. Essentially, the attractive or repulsive force that characterizes the energetic interplay of atomic particles in electromagnetism is the same Qi at work in the interaction between animals and human beings in their surrounding environment.

These fundamental invisible forces of nature, which modern scientists have for decades attempted to show as the different manifestations of a single, underlying force, are indeed the various aspects of the ancients' own Unified Field Theory called Tai Qi (or "great energy"). In fact, to a certain extent, we can say that physics has created formulas to interpret how Qi manifests itself in the physical world, or how the physical world is itself the manifestation of invisible life force energy.

Qi and Manmade Sources of Electromagnetism

Feng Shui is a natural discipline that studies the interaction between various energy fields existing in nature. However, its primary focus is on how the human energy field interacts with the surrounding natural environment.

In modern days, man-made sources of electromagnetism have contributed to the increasing energy imbalance of our environment. Massive electric power poles and transformers have been investigated as causes of long-term and sometimes fatal health problems. Large factories discharging pollution into the air and water are some of the most dangerous features of our industrial and technological era. Among other offenders, freeways and airports also contribute to air and noise pollution. Although useful in improving the quality of our lives, these modern developments often do not contribute to supporting the balance in the life force of our environment, and consequently ours.

Such hazards were not factors in Feng Shui practices thousands of years ago, simply because they didn't exist. Reckoning with these enormous modern sources of unhealthy energy, contemporary Feng Shui consultants realize that in many cases, especially in urban and industrial communities, there is little that an individual can do other than to relocate.

How Do We Know It's There? Can We See It?

Let's try this brief exercise: Sit down comfortably, and shake your hands and arms for a few seconds to stimulate blood circulation. You can also massage the inside of your palms. Now put your palms together. Try to clear your mind of any distracting thoughts. Focus your awareness on the space between your hands, and be aware of any sensation between the two palms.

Now very slowly pull your hands apart about ten inches, palms still facing each other. Once they are ten inches apart, pause for a few seconds, and then slowly push your palms back together.

Did you notice any feeling? Was there any resistance to pressure, tingling, or sense of warmth in the center of your palms? Even if barely noticeable? What you are sensing is the intensity of your energy field radiating from your hands.

This is your Qi: It's your personal energy which is different from everyone else's.

Simple, isn't it? As you practice this brief exercise at different times during the day, you may notice that the sensation may be stronger or weaker depending on such factors as whether you had a good night's rest or whether you are tired from lack of sleep or excessive stress.

Qi and Feng Shui

The concept of Qi is also at the heart of Feng Shui. In fact, knowing how Earth's Qi affects the environment and human physiology is essential to gaining a proper understanding not only of Feng Shui, but also of the entire world of subtle energy. Simply put, Qi is the life force contained in all physical matter, from inanimate objects to human beings. Some forms of matter contain more energy than others and some energy may be stronger, but ultimately everything is life-force energy, and everything interacts with everything else.

When we decide to move the position of a door or a window in a house, for example, we may at first create a sense of disorientation, as the original pattern of Qi has been altered. The new pattern will gradually become more stable, and we will adapt to it progressively as we begin to feel comfortable again. When a change seems to create "better" Feng Shui, this means that an area was earlier affected by obstructed or stagnating Qi and it is now experiencing a new energy dynamic, a freeing of the energy that was previously trapped. This type of change manifests a much greater sense of ease and comfort within a space.

氣 ： 乘風則散
界水則止

"Qi disperses when riding on the wind and stalls when reaching the water's edge." **The understanding of this sentence, contained in one of the most ancient Feng Shui texts (***Zhang Shu*** or ***Book of Burial,*** approximately A.D. 300), is at the very core of the understanding of how the life-force energy operates in the environment that surrounds us.**

Therefore, it is important for us to live and work in areas where there is beneficial Qi. This is why the ancients hired a geomancer to review a site and to advise them prior to construction. The sages knew that interactions between Qi, time, and space have a direct effect on our lives, and selecting a site where the Qi is "ill," or choosing the wrong building orientation or an inappropriate time for construction, could cause an energy imbalance that could have poor effects on one's well-being and on one's journey through life in general.

Feng Shui = Wind and Water

Literally translated as *wind* and *water*, *Feng Shui* derives its name from these two elements. The pattern of movement of Qi is found in the dynamic of these primary elements of the natural environment. Qi is carried by the wind, and it is stopped by water at its edge, just to be returned through the water's gentle movement.

The environment and its features affect the health of human beings indirectly because of their influence on the movement of Qi. For example, light breezes carry good energy, while strong winds break it and disperse it. Clear, flowing water absorbs and stores Qi before it slowly releases it in the form of negatively charged ions, which foster health and well-being. On the other hand, features such as dirty or stagnant water pollute the life force and have unfavorable effects on our health.

69

The Chinese characters for *feng* (wind) and *shui* (water). The name of the discipline, Feng Shui, is directly related to the sentence appearing in the previous illustration, and it implies the importance of understanding how Qi operates in the study of the discipline.

A popular Chinese proverb explains that a healthy living environment can alter the personality, attitude, and health positively and can help us excel in many other aspects of life. By applying Feng Shui to our architecture and interior design, we are going to improve our living and working environments, and consequently our lives.

The Three Powers

Qi is traditionally divided into three main kingdoms, also called Three Powers:

Heavenly Qi can be described as energy raining down from heaven and its interaction with the Earth, i.e., solar and lunar influences on sea tides, weather, time, and cycles of changes in the environment (the seasons). Though we cannot observe Heavenly Qi itself, we can see its effects on the planet's topography. It is also primarily responsible for the element of time in Feng Shui practice, which will be discussed in the Advanced Theories section.

Earthly Qi is the planet's response to the heavens through the features of its topography. It is seen as energy radiating up from the Earth. It affects all aspects of the natural environment, such as mountains, rivers, forests, deserts, and other terrestrial formations. It is primarily responsible for the elements of building orientation, direction, and alignment in Feng Shui practice. We consider Earthly Qi when we examine structures made by man, including other terrestrial variables such as color, light, sound, and movement. Common physical objects are also subject to Earthly Qi, including furniture, clothes, cars, etc. Once an inanimate object is created, its life-force energy immediately starts aging and cannot be replenished. In Feng Shui we describe this as Qi going from a Yang state to a Yin state. This is why old belongings and antique pieces of furniture can project an impression of 'sucking' away the life force.

Human Qi encompasses the personal life force of the individual as expressed in the human body, mind, and soul. Energy meridians, thoughts, karma, and the destinies of individuals are all attributes of this life force. Religious backgrounds, social classes, cultural influences, education, and family history all play a role in shaping one's Human Qi. Each individual body is created from specific vibrations, or "energetic notes" of Earthly Qi that resonates with the spirit that inhabits such body. Your hair may be brown or blond because of physical inheritance from your parents' genes (DNA), but your DNA and your parents DNA actually share the same Qi 'note' for creating the color of your hair. Each individual's phenotype is different from others because it has been generated from a distinct and unique collection of energy 'notes'.

Technically, the physical body is considered as being made of Earthly Qi. It starts aging immediately after it is created because of a depletion of its original "essence;" however, its overall nature is very different from that of a physical object. It is a lot more complex because of the activities taking place simultaneously inside it, and its ability to contain several different kinds of life-force energies to coordinate all these functions. However this "life essence" with which we are born can be preserved, therefore slowing down the aging process, with a proper diet, meditation, and physical exercises such as various types of *Qigong* and *Taiji*. Once the life-force is preserved, the cells will renew themselves and the aging process will slow down.

Qi and the *I Ching*

As mentioned earlier, Feng Shui knowledge, along with other sciences and philosophies, is derived from the *I Ching*, which in turn is based on the study of mathematical combinations of the Eight Trigrams discovered by the ancient sages (Chapter 1). *I Ching* is an ancient text that is said to contain the secret wisdom of the universe and in the Chinese culture it is as esteemed as the Bible is in the Western culture.

The underlying theory is based on the observation of nature and its cycles and how these affect human lives. After observing changes in nature and in people long enough, it is possible to recognize patterns that repeat themselves in cycles. This is as true for the changes in people lives as it is for the cycles of the sun, moon, and seasons. Understanding the patterns is a sure way to forecast outcomes and, in the long run, to be able to take advantage of these changes. The purpose is not to be pushed blindly through a life of misery but to improve fortune by learning to move and to rest according to the direction of the changes in the cycle that is ahead.

Changes are the seeds of life; there is no life without change. It is through change that we enter each subsequent stage of life. It is by knowing when changes are coming and making the best of them that we learn from this experience called life.

The book of the *I Ching* is composed of 64 hexagrams, each of which represents a different cycle and timing. These hexagrams are the results of all possible combinations of the Eight Trigrams (8 x 8 = 64). Each trigram is a symbol composed of three horizontal lines (*tri* = three; *gramma* = drawing, writing, record) of which the upper line represents Heavenly Qi, the middle represents Human Qi, and the lower represents Earthly Qi.

When observing trigrams we notice that they are composed of continuous lines (—) or broken lines (– –). The continuous line has a

Yang energy polarity, and the broken line has a Yin energy polarity (see more about Yin and Yang in the next chapter). Each individual trigram has a unique form of energy; none is like the other because it is composed of either Yin or Yang in the Heavenly Qi, Yin or Yang in the Human Qi, and Yin or Yang in the Earthly Qi.

The study of the meaning and effects of these energy patterns on the human life runs throughout the history of Chinese science, literature, and philosophy. In his last days, after spending all his life studying the hidden code of the Book of Changes, Confucius himself declared, "If I had fifty more years to live, I would spend them all studying the *I Ching*."

Visible and Invisible Qi

When planning to undertake the task of designing a building, it is important to keep in mind that the building you will eventually create is not detached from its surrounding environment, nor can its internal energy be examined without taking into account changes in the cosmic energy or in the energy of the planet.

This step involves looking at two different aspects of the life-force energy (Qi) commonly defined as the *visible* and the *invisible* (or *seen* and *unseen*, or *tangible* and *intangible*) *Qi*.

Visible Qi

Visible, or tangible, Qi is defined this way not because it can actually be seen by the naked eye, but rather because its patterns are predictable from the positioning of tangible objects around us.

For example, a house at the end of a T-shaped intersection receives the strong effects of Qi from the road facing it. Although most people cannot actually see the Qi assaulting the building, we can recognize its disrupting effects on the building by observing the building's appearance and/or interviewing the inhabitants about their experiences during the time they have been living or working in that building.

The same can be said regarding the interior of a building. For example, it is common knowledge nowadays that having two doors aligned is not a favorable Feng Shui feature. What many do not understand is that between these two doors a subtle draft is created, and this draft pulls the Qi in one door and pushes it out the other. The draft causes a fast Qi movement, therefore not giving enough time to impart its beneficial effects to the room.

With years of experience, a good consultant can begin to develop a subtle new sensory ability, and in the long term the pattern of Qi can become visible to a well-trained and experienced eye.

This is the most ancient technique of Feng Shui masters, which they were already aware of five thousand years ago. This approach is what is commonly known as "form knowledge," often referred to in the modern era as the Form School.

Invisible Qi

When we talk about invisible Qi, or unseen influences, we are referring to very different circumstances. The invisible Qi has to do with a combination of Heaven (Cosmic) Qi and Earth Qi that can become sealed inside a building at the moment of construction. In a sense, this combination becomes the DNA of the building. When a Feng Shui expert examines the energy distribution inside a building, he or she can determine accurate information and make predictions about the effects on the inhabitants. This can explain why a building that is apparently beautiful and in a beneficial environment can bring misfortune to the people living in it. It can also inform us as to how a building situated at the end of a "T" intersection (potentially a very inauspicious configuration) can actually bring great financial prosperity to its owners. Such a situation, although very rare, is still possible. I, however, recommend that beginners leave this type of determination to an expert.

The study of invisible Qi involves the use of the date of the construction of the building and its orientation. With these two data, it is possible to derive the Heaven Qi and the Earth Qi. To effectively determine a building's orientation, it is mandatory to use a Lo Pan compass, and to use Magnetic North as a reference.

The study of invisible Qi in Feng Shui has been labeled the Compass School.

In Traditional Feng Shui we learn that both of these aspects, Visible and Invisible, should be considered. When used properly, one can balance or enhance the other. Since Feng Shui began to spread in the Western culture, a dichotomy between Form School and Compass school emerged, making one an alternative to the other. This couldn't be further from the truth of the matter. When the differences between visible and invisible Qi are understood, it is clear that one cannot be considered without the other. To execute a complete analysis of a building, both are essential.

Chapter 4

UNDERLYING
FENG SHUI THEORIES

Traditional Feng Shui is constituted of certain important principals and theories that have evolved from the study of the Eight Trigrams and the *I Ching*. A good understanding of these principals is thus a prerequisite for those who would seriously practice Feng Shui. The major theories we derive from the *I Ching* deal with:

- Yin/Yang Polarity
- The Five Elements
- The Eight Trigrams
- Qi Flow in the Environment

From these basic principals more advanced and complex theoretical combinations, practices, and interpretations, or schools (*pai*) have evolved. Among them are the following:

- *Luan Tou Pai* - Mountain Top (Form School; *Xing Jia*)
- *Li-Qi Pai* - Qi Regulating (Compass School)
- *Ba Zhai Ming-Jing Pai*—Bright Mirror of Eight Mansions, Directions, or Houses
- *San Yuan Pai* - Three Cycles, Periods, or Principles, or Triple Primaries
- *Xung Kung (Xuan Kong Fei Xing) Pai*—Mysterious Void (time-space)/Flying Stars
- *San He Pai* - Triple Combination

Each school specializes in a particular aspect of Feng Shui and follows a slightly different application from the next. Although these are often referred as "schools," each of them looks at the different aspects of the whole. Just like a doctor who has studied Traditional medicine and Oriental medicine, the more a consultant knows and the more experiences he or she is, the more information can be collected during an analysis, and the more effective his or her advice.

For the purposes of this book we will focus on the opposite polarities of Yin and Yang, the transformational cycle of the Five Elements, an introduction to the Eight Trigrams and the "visible" Qi flow in the environment.

Yin and Yang: The Universe in Perfect Balance

"Two things, one origin,
But different names,
Whose identity is mystery.
Mystery of all mysteries!
The door to the hidden."

Lao Tzu, *Tao Te Ching*

When we look at Qi more closely, we find it is composed of two main polarities, Yin and Yang. Observing the well-known *Tai Qi* symbol (sometimes translated as *Great Energy*), one sees how Yin and Yang create a graphic visualization of the entire universe, considered in its opposite polarities, in perfect harmony with two soft, flowing forms embracing each other and smoothly following a clockwise movement.

Representing opposite and complementary forces existent throughout nature, Yin and Yang are the warp and woof of the universe. Everything is made of Yin and Yang, and they cannot be separated, but when one is created, the other automatically comes to existence. Balance can only exist with an equal pairing of opposites, compensating and balancing each other. For every Yin,

The *Tai Qi* symbol, with its Yin and Yang dichotomy, is a graphic expression of the law of constant change and perfect balance in the universe.

there is always a corresponding aspect of Yang, and for every element of Yang, there is always an aspect of Yin.

This pattern of balance, which is the operative principal of the entire universe, is derived from the observations of nature in such opposed and yet complimentary elements as hot and cold, dry and humid, light and dark, and so on.

Attributes of Yin and Yang

On the next page are some of the traditional associations acknowledged as expressions of Yin and Yang. I invite you to experience them for yourself and to discover more of this balance in your daily life.

The Twelve Principals of Yin and Yang

Following are 12 principles of Yin and Yang which were given by the legendary Yellow Emperor. Along with each of them I have included a commentary.

YANG	YIN
Heaven	Earth
Sun	Moon
Spring, Summer	Autumn, Winter
Male	Female
Heat, Warmth	Cold, Coldness
Dryness	Moisture
Larger, Powerful	Smaller, Weaker
The Upper Part	The Lower Part
Fire	Water, Rain
Movement	Quiescence
Day	Night
The Left Side	The Right Side
The East and South	The West and North
The Back of the body	The Front of the body
(from head to tail bone)	(from chest to belly)
Hours between midnight and noon	Hours between noon and midnight
Repletion	Depletion
Clarity	Murkiness
Incipience	Development
Destruction	Conservation
Aggressiveness	Responsiveness
Expansion	Contraction
Soul	Body

Table 1. Yin and Yangs Attributes

1) That which produces and composes the universe is the *Tao* (or *Dao*), the undivided oneness or ultimate nothingness.

The Tao, also known as "the Way," is the cosmic pattern of actions and reactions through which life unfolds, a constant cycle of change that includes both highs and lows. Everything existing in the universe is constituted of self-balancing opposites that keep life flowing and are visible to us as changes.

The sun rises in the East, crosses the sky, and sets in the West, disappearing from our view. When we first saw what happened as babies, we may have thought, "That's it; it's over." Then the following morning, it rose again in the East, crossed the sky, and set in the West again. Soon we began to understand change as we learned that it is a consistent element of the cycles of nature.

79

Later, in school, we learned that the Earth rotates on its axis while traveling in a elliptical path around the sun, and our lives are regulated by this cosmic cycle. Most of us get up in the morning after sunrise and go to sleep at night after dark. Our lives, economy and travel plans are all regulated by this pattern. Since I live in California and my parents live in Italy, I do not call them at six in the evening and wonder why they are sleeping. I know that where they are it's the middle of the night, and the sun hasn't "risen" there yet.

Our habits are developed with our understanding of the way things work best, and we normally go with the flow because we acknowledge that going against such overwhelming laws of nature can be uncomfortable and is generally unnecessary.

2) The Tao is polarized as a correspondent set of complementary opposites. Yang is the active pole of the cosmos, and Yin is the passive pole.

Everything in nature has its counterpart; the active is inextricably married to its opposite, the passive; the left to the right; the day and the night; the upper and the lower; etc. This principle is fundamental to the existence of life. It is the interaction of opposites that creates the dynamic fluctuation of change, without which there would be no life.

3) Yang and Yin are opposites, and each fulfills and complements the other.

When Yang is strong, Yin is weak in proportion. When Yang is weak, Yin will be proportionately weaker. The polarized energies adjust to maintain balance.

4) Everything in the universe is a complex aggregate of universal energy, composed of balanced proportions of Yin and Yang.

From a grain of sand to a galaxy, everything in the universe is composed of Yang and Yin in perfect balance to ensure the dynamic creation of life. This is the rule of the dichotomy behind the graphic Tai Qi (Yin/Yang) symbol.

5) **All beings and things are in a dynamic state of change and transformation. Nothing in the universe is absolutely static or completed; all is in unceasing motion because balanced polarization, the source of being, is without beginning and without end.**

The alternating flow from one aspect to the opposite and back again is what creates continuous change and keeps life moving and evolving. It is in the dynamism of the change that we enjoy being alive.

6) **Yin and Yang attract one another.**

They are opposites, but drawn to complete each other by joining. It is this continual tension that creates and sustains life.

7) **Nothing is entirely Yin or entirely Yang: all phenomena are composed of both Yin and Yang.**

Although some things may appear to be entirely Yin or entirely Yang, the corresponding opposite exists in a balanced proportion, although it may not be as obvious. It is in the nature of change that, when something reaches the extreme at one end of the spectrum, it rolls over to the other end. When the winter is at its peak and seems to grow coldest, the seeds of spring are just around the corner, ready to sprout, and life is created again. So in the peak of the hot summer we can often sense the approaching fall, especially in the moist air of the evening.

8) **Nothing is neutral. All phenomena are composed of varying and unequal proportions of Yin and Yang.**

Nothing is neutral because when something exhibits Yin, its counterpart Yang appears, and vice versa. Beyond appearance, the seeds of change are within everything.

9) **The force of attraction between Yin and Yang is greater when the difference between them is greater, and it is smaller when the difference between them is smaller.**

The more extreme the imbalance, the more Yin and Yang attract each other. The less extreme, the weaker the attraction.

10) Like activities repel one another. The closer the similarities between two entities of the same polarity, the greater the repulsion.

Similarities don't bring balance. Only differences can, since what is missing in one will be present in the other. Highly similar elements cannot complete each other as opposites do.

11) At the extremes of their expression, Yin produces Yang, and Yang produces Yin.

When reaching the extreme of their strength, Yin and Yang become their opposites. This concept is also visually expressed by the Tai Qi symbol. When looking at the top of the Yang half, we notice that the seed of the opposite is inside the fullest part. That might be, for example, the seed of winter in the midst of summer heat. Likewise in the midst of cold winter, the seed of spring is ready to sprout.

Another example, which I find very amusing, refers specifically to the Western mind. One of our favorite pursuits is the achievement of perfection. The theory is that the more "perfect" you are in your thoughts, actions, and results, the better person you are. In the theory of Yin and Yang, however, when you attempt to approach this kind of perfection, all you do is set yourself up for typically unexpected mistakes and problems that force you to work even harder.

In ancient times, Italian architects and artist were very familiar with this concept and very often one will find hidden in some corner of a masterpiece an unexpected flaw, either a mistake in proportion or an ugly detail. For artists of yore, this error was a way to make a masterpiece less then perfect so that it would endure forever.

12) All beings are Yang in the center and Yin on the surface.

The powerful growing drive of Yang is often hidden inside, while the exterior is more placid and has a Yin nature. Our planet has an apparent passive and static surface, where mountains survive seemingly intact for eons as do the oceans. However, deep in their centers there is heat and an ever-changing chemical transformation. Polarity is similar in the human body, where the inner functions and continuous chemical transformations remain hidden and invisible while the surface of the body reveals little of what is happening deep inside.

Yin/Yang and Natural Cycles

By exercising our ability to understanding the principal of opposite-yet-complimentary balance, we can see within it all of nature's cycles. For example, contained within the solar cycle of a day is the natural interaction and progression of Yin and Yang. In fact, the Yin and Yang polarities were originally described in terms of sunshine and shade. At the darkest hour before sunrise and during daybreak, the sun releases positive energy waves of light (Yang polarity) into the atmosphere where they engage in a dance with the opposite energy waves of darkness (Yin polarity). Just as the sun (a Yang element) rises and travels toward its highest point in the sky, the force of Yang rises symbolically to the top of the Tai Qi symbol. By noon, the sun reaches its zenith, and its natural progression is to decline toward the horizon, which reflects a downward and falling movement of Yin polarity.

The same Yin/Yang interaction and progression occurs in the lunar cycle, which is the most significant Yin element. Figuratively beginning at the top of the Tai Qi symbol and following a clockwise movement, the moon reaches its peak at the bottom of the symbol, precisely when the sun's radiation is at its nadir. As the moon wanes and the sun radiates again, the sun once again begins its upward symbolic journey toward the top of the Tai Qi symbol (Yang), and a new day begins.

This principal of interaction between Yin and Yang is evidenced in all other cycles of nature, such as the seasons and life and death. I invite you to investigate the natural world and experience it thoughtfully. In the rhythmic dance of life, the infinite cycles of nature, are always in balance; they do not strive to do this, they simply are.

Applying Yin and Yang to Our Environment

It is fascinating to study the natural world and see the way nature maintains a balance between these two energies, while our manmade world often suffers from their imbalance.

To create harmony in our lives is to create as natural a balance of the Yin and Yang factors as possible in every aspect of our environment and within our manmade structures. For example, aspects of the environment that are excessively Yang create stress and instability, and those that are strongly Yin foster stagnation and depression. Therefore, darkness should be balanced with light, coolness with heat, humidity with dryness, complexity with simplicity, and so forth.

To create balance, we can apply the unifying principles of Yin and Yang. Since everything in nature is composed of energy, where that energy is overly active it can be balanced with features containing greater passivity, and where too passive, it can be balanced with more active features.

The ancient theories of the polarity of Yin and Yang were applied throughout the Chinese culture. All theories used in Feng Shui today maintain these principles of polarity and apply them in a more or less direct manner. Observation of the natural environment and the application of Yin and Yang principals to the "visible Qi" flow constitute the most ancient part of Feng Shui, often defined as the "Form School."

Five Elements: Constant Energy Transformation

What is commonly defined as Qi is really the dynamic biological energy that supports us physically, emotionally and spiritually. Ancient and modern Feng Shui masters acknowledge that every element in the physical world is constituted of this ever-transforming life force. All elements have their own unique energy frequencies, they are all manifested as the infinite variety of matter, and they are all accompanied by sound, smell, sight, taste, and feeling, which we interpret for the most part through our senses.

The energy contained in such elements cannot be created or destroyed, but instead modulates or transforms its intensity and frequency following natural cycles.

The ancients broke down this infinite transformation into five basic agents or phases, associated (for the sake of study and memorization) with the elements that make up our physical world: wood, fire, earth, metal, and water. The transformation of these

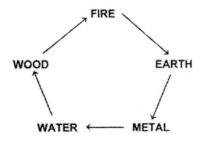

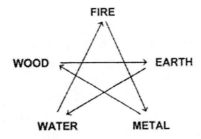

The Five Elements cycle. The five stages of transformation can be remembered easily by associating them with the physical elements. Above: the productive cycle of transformation. Below: the dominating cycle. Changing a dominating cycle into a productive cycle by using the missing element helps re-establish balance.

elements reflects the transformation of energy in a continuous regenerating cycle.

Much as electricity flowing through a conduit is seen only by way of its physical manifestations in appliances and lighting fixtures, so is Qi essentially invisible and intangible, manifesting itself as the Five Elements and their attendant cycles of transformation. Thus the Five Elements Theory enables us to visualize Qi through cycles of transformation that affect all the physical phenomena of our universe. To achieve a complete mastery of the energies working in our environment and within us, however, experience and the application of theory in practice is essential.

The Productive Cycle

The Five Elements undergo a series of transformations that represent the productive cycle of nature: Water feeds and nourishes wood, which in turn burns, producing fire. Fire creates ashes, which nourish the earth in whose womb metal is formed. Finally, metal's coolness condenses surface air, precipitating water. The entire process of creation is contained within this cycle, and Feng Shui masters therefore strive to ensure a balance of the Five Elements in terms of a harmonious relationship between buildings, people, and the factor of time.

In the analysis of a structure's energy, practical application of the Five Elements Theory is necessary to establish harmony. Thus, if one finds that an element is lacking or unavailable, one can introduce a color, for example, that has the same energy frequency in the electromagnetic spectrum. For example, the element of wood can be replaced by various shades of green; fire can be substituted with various shades of red; earth with beige, tan, ocher, yellow, or brown shades; metal with white, gray, and silver; and water with various shade of blue and black.

The compatibility of human beings with our surrounding environment is characterized and determined by the Five Elements and their attendant energy transformations. The correlation between an element and its influences on our human/environment interaction can be subtle or obvious, but it is well worth understanding.

The Destructive Cycle

Whenever elements in the productive chain are lacking, an opposite reaction occurs: a destructive cycle is set in motion. In lay terms, a destructive cycle means that the overall energy is not balanced and creates a potentially negative influence on those exposed to it. In terms of energy transformation, the elements are no longer symbiotic, they have become mutually opposed and they negate one another: Water extinguishes fire; fire melts metal; metal chops wood; wood pierces earth; earth muddies water and prevents it from flowing. This cycle of opposition and negation has a strong impact on people's well being and it can bring about serious health problems or other difficulties if it is not corrected.

Correcting the Destructive Cycle

To correct a destructive cycle, one can introduce a symbiotic element to neutralize two opposing elements. For example, if water is extinguishing fire, wood can be added to feed the fire. Similarly, if fire is melting metal, earth will reestablish a supportive ground for metal to thrive again. Thus, water will nourish wood if metal attacks it; fire will fertilize earth if wood depletes it; and metal will channel and protect water if earth dams it up.

The purpose of correcting the destructive cycle is to increase the favorable effects and eliminate the negative effects on the human physiology.

The ability to analyze the energy of a structure according to the Five Element Theory and to know how and where to balance the elements is a vital part of mastering the art of advanced Feng Shui and it is clearly the subject of life-long study.

Connection between Yin and Yang and Five Elements

The cycle of transformation of the Five Elements can also be read in terms of Yin and Yang and seen in the Tai Qi symbol. Symbolically, deep, flowing water resides at the bottom of the symbol. Water feeds wood, which grows in an upward movement toward the sky. As wood catches fire and burns, the energy reaches the apex of the symbol at its top (like the sun in the midday sky). As fire consumes, producing ashes and nourishing earth, the downward cycle begins. From earth's womb, metal is created, and as water is formed from metal's coolness, the energy completes its cycle and returns to the bottom of the symbol where a new cycle starts all over again.

Understanding how to correct unbalanced energies through

the Yin/Yang and Five Elements theories becomes especially important when dealing with *Sha*, or polluted Qi. It is also used extensively in advanced Feng Shui applications, as well as in Chinese astrology and in Traditional Chinese Medicine.

Eight Trigrams and Luo Shu Sequences

Thus far, we have learned that Qi is composed of balanced yet opposing polarities, which evolve and change through a cycle of Five Element transformations. Now we will see how all these aspects link together and how we can read them in the natural environment.

The Five Elements divide into a series of polarities, some Yin, others Yang. The various permutations of these polarities form the Eight Trigrams, representing a simple, but effective method for tracking the manifestation of energies in the physical world.

The Eight Trigrams, discovered by the legendary founder of Chinese culture Fu Xi through his observation of the natural environment, are the basic components of the *I Ching's* 64 hexagrams.

Each trigram consists of an ordered combination of three lines that represent life-force energy as it is defined by Yin/Yang theory. Again, Yang energy is represented by a continuous line and Yin by a broken line. The trigrams are read from bottom to top and they represent three levels of energy: The upper line represents heaven or celestial energy radiating down on us, called Heavenly Qi. The middle line represents man, or the human interaction with what is above and below which is called Human Qi. The lower line represents earth or the terrestrial energy radiating up to the heavens, called Earthy Qi.

As the basis of various advanced theories, each trigram is assigned several associations.

Yin/Yang, Five Elements, and Eight Trigrams

In terms of Yin/Yang and Five Elements theories, the trigrams are defined as follows:

Trigram	Polarity	Element	Direction
Qian	Yang	Metal	Northwest
Kun	Yin	Earth	Southwest
Zhen	Yang	Wood	East
Kan	Yang	Water	North
Gen	Yang	Earth	Northeast
Xun	Yin	Wood	Southeast
Li	Yin	Fire	South
Dui	Yin	Metal	West

Table 2. **The Eight Trigrams and their associated polarities, elements, and compass directions**

As the Post-Heaven Order illustrates on the next page, the trigrams share certain elements and have opposite polarities:

Gen and Kun: both are earth; one is Yang, and one is Yin

Qian and Dui: both are metal; one is Yang, and one is Yin

Zhen and Xun: both are wood; one is Yang, and one is Yin

Kan and Li have respectively Yang and Yin polarities although one is water, and the other is fire. They are at the extreme high and low points of the Yin/Yang symbol, naturally opposing and complementing each other.

Individual trigrams are generally associated with heaven and earth, fire and water, mountain and lake, wind and thunder. These associations refer to the *quantum Qi* component inherent in each trigram. The effects are not seen in a single finite situation, but in the combinations of various trigrams. For example, in the Eight Mansions Theory, where the house trigram relates to the occupants' trigram, or in Xuan Kong System, where the trigram of the current year relates to the trigram of the house and its internal energy distribution.

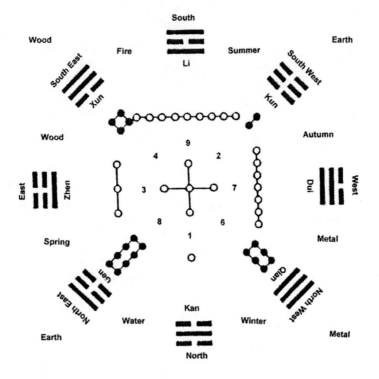

The Post-Heaven order of trigrams and their association with directions and elements, as derived from the Luo Shu diagram.

Chapter 5

SELECTING THE RIGHT SITE

Ancient Chinese Feng Shui books often depict the best building-site layout as an "armchair": an open expanse of land bounded by gently flowing water and surrounded on three sides by mountains with its back supported by a peak, with minor ranges on the sides.

This illustration suggests that, ideally, buildings should respect a concept referred to as the *Black Tortoise*, which means that they should be supported from behind. The *Black Tortoise* can be a mountain or a tall line of trees.

Minor supporting elements should be present on the sides of buildings: such elements are traditionally known respectively as *Green Dragon* and *White Tiger*. The *Green Dragon* and the *White Tiger* could be provided by trees, bushes, adjacent buildings, or perhaps by a garage or pool-house in contemporary living.

Buildings should also have an open frontage. The concept of facing a street with unobtrusive traffic is traditionally referred to as *Red Phoenix* because of its dynamic potential as opposed to the placid stability of the *Tortoise* at the back.

The reason behind this concept is that an unsupported building lacks the protection from the winds that blow excessive or unfavorable Qi against it or can blow away its positive Qi. The support and protection at the back and sides retain this precious life-force energy while leaving the front open to receive more positive life force and to direct it toward the entrance. As an example of an imbalance, consider yourself sitting in a chair that has been de-

When the traditional "armchair" mountain layout is not available, it can be replicated artificially with trees, bushes, adjacent buildings, or a garage to protect the back and sides from the wind that would otherwise disperse the ambient life-force energy.

signed to be a work of art, perhaps with one arm much higher then the other or with only one arm. My experience is that in such situations where the two arms are not balanced, the sitting posture becomes uncomfortable and the effect is unsettling.

Searching for the perfect environment nowadays is often not the easiest way to proceed in selecting a site. With this consideration in mind, how can we evaluate a site when it does not meet these requirements? Here is what I suggest.

My Land Evaluation

When designing a project, the first step is to evaluate the plot of land where the building will stand. Constructing a sound building from scratch is easier than remodeling, simply because there's more flexibility in terms of what can be done. Remodeling can be more of a structural challenge when one is faced with reorganizing and modifying preexisting conditions. This is true in terms of both physical structure and internal energy distribution.

A building left unprotected and exposed at the back and sides is more likely to suffer a depletion of life-force energy that can bring about negative consequences in regard to the well being of the occupants (Leesburg, VA).

When I visit a site, I walk the entire stretch of land and observe. What do I look for? I observe the pattern of visible Qi and the effects it has on the land.

I observe the positions of natural features, such as mountains and creeks, and how they interact with the wind. I look at the positions of the surrounding streets and observe their behavior to see if they caress the land or dominate it aggressively. I look at the location of other buildings nearby and witness whether their effects are supportive or damaging. I consider where plants and water could be better situated after the completion of the project so that I can design the project with them in mind.

I walk all the way around the lot and also observe the center, so that I can view the current land formation and the elevation of the ground and to consider the lot's shape. After I have found a location that I feel is the most favorable site for the building, I stand still, breathe deeply, and meditate.

I imagine standing inside the building as if it were already built. I envision the building around me, and I feel how the resident Qi will affect the building upon its completion. Sometimes I will suddenly become aware of something I didn't consider before, and

93

I'll move to another spot to check further. I may realize that, although the building's position works just fine, a little landscaping is necessary to improve it. In most cases, I know that I have hit the "right spot" for a building when I feel overwhelmed with a sense of serenity and peacefulness.

Natural Environment

The study of the natural environment for a *Yang* house siting goes back to back with *Yin* house siting. While Yang House Feng Shui refers to buildings for Yang people, or the living, Yin House Feng Shui addresses the location of grave sites, literally, houses for the deceased. In fact, it is believed that through the genes and the genetic life force, the location of ancestors in gravesites chosen and designed according to favorable Feng Shui principles will have a positive effect on their descendants. These principles were commonly applied throughout several powerful Chinese dynasties, in order to support their successors and ensure the continuity of power.

Most of the theories about tracking visible Qi for Yang house purposes were originally adapted from Yin house practices. However, not all of them were appropriate for the houses of the living. Some of these theories are strictly related to Yin houses and have nothing to offer Yang houses. In contemporary literature, many authors who aren't entirely familiar with the differences between the two tend to offer information that is actually inappropriate for the Yang house, which can cause confusion.

Dragon Mountains vs. Dead Mountains

Some ancient books refer to the so-called "Dragon Mountain." Ideally, they advise never to build "on the back of the dragon" or "under the dragon's mouth" or "on the dragon's tail."

What is a "dragon mountain?"

Just as the ancient Chinese often referred to the emperor as "the Dragon," a man who distinguishes himself from the rest, a

The skyline of a mountain rich in life-force energy should resemble the back of a dormant dragon. In this case, the mountain overlooks the water, while the flat area in between becomes an ideal place to build a house (China).

dragon mountain is one that has exceptional life-force energy by comparison to others. Here are some ways to determine if a mountain is a dragon mountain:

- Observe its outline or skyline; ideally, it should resemble the back of a dormant dragon or, in other words, a series of soft curves.
- Observe the quality of plants that grow on its sides; they should be vivid green and healthy, with oily leaves.
- Observe the quality of the soil; it should be healthy and rich in Qi.
- Observe the presence of "dragon veins," or smooth ridges under which the Earth Qi runs.
- Observe the presence of "dragon eyes," which are flat areas between the mountain's raised lines where Qi can gather. These dragon eyes are excellent areas to locate a house or a group of houses or, if large enough, an entire town.

On the other hand, a dead mountain can also be described by observing its features. These include a harsh and pointy shape, dry and exhausted soil, exposed rocks, pale color, and a lack of vegetation. All are characteristics of a mountain that has exhausted its life force and would therefore qualify as a "dead dragon".

Beautiful mountains that lack dragon eyes could be considered "false dragons." In this case, although the good characteristics are there, there is no flat land where the Qi can gather and buildings can be constructed. Therefore, although the Qi is there, it cannot be taken advantage of.

The dryness of land is a clear symptom that the life-force energy has been exhausted. In Matera, Italy, the famous *sassi* were cave dwellings and structures were carved into the rock of a plateau is an example of an area which, over the centuries, has progressively been abandoned as a place of homes, possibly as a natural consequence of the exhaustion of Qi in the surrounding environment.

Reading the Life-Force Energy in the Site: Yang Qi and Yin Qi

In ancient meteorological terms, high pressure or rising air is considered Yang Qi, while sinking air due to low pressure is defined as Yin Qi. The same can be said about the quality of Qi flowing in and around a building. As a rule of thumb, a home should be at all times filled with Yang Qi, or living and vibrant energy, while Yin Qi should be avoided, as it is only favorable for Yin houses (of final rest), the dwellings of the deceased.

It is also helpful to remember that in Feng Shui, balance is often the key. In the West we are often tempted to think that if one is good, then a hundred is a hundred times as good. This is not always so in Feng Shui. While we like to have Yang energy around us for the majority of the time, a "super Yang" environment is going to be too much for us and it could be its own downfall. Just as in the Tai Qi (*t'ai ch'i*) Yin-Yang symbol in which the Yang half rises to reach its highest peak and then becomes Yin, so can excessive Yang features turn into damaging Yin features.

For example, living close to the element of water is very energizing and positive because of the strong Yang Qi of the element; however, the Yang energy of a house built right on the beach overlooking the ocean will be overwhelmed, and the house could experience such Yin effects as excessive humidity, dampness, mold, rot, etc.

Checklist for Selecting a Site

When selecting a site, make sure to evaluate and, if possible, adjust for these elements:

- Land Elevation
- Lot Size and Shape
- Wind and Water Patterns
- Urban Environment and Manmade Structures
- Landscape Design and Garden Arrangement
- Sources of Negative Qi, or *Sha Qi* (also spelled *Shar)*

The same points are also to be evaluated when planning a remodeling or a simple landscape redesign. These are all factors contributing to a desirable environment that will enhance the quality of a house. The flow of Qi in the environment is to a home what food is to the body. Just as our bodies thrive on fresh and healthy nutrition, our homes benefit from the healthy flow of Qi. Conversely, just as our bodies are poisoned by a diet filled with junk food, our home stagnates with negative Qi, or *Sha Qi*. Thus, assessing positive Qi, or *Sheng Qi*, flow is the first step towards a proper Feng Shui analysis.

Land Elevation

Some of the situations described in this section are very common and yet not always easy to correct, as they may involve leveling a large portion of land and often require the construction of expensive retaining walls. However, while selecting and purchasing land, these cases can be kept in mind to help you understand which property offers you the optimal potential for future construction.

If possible, the house should be built on level ground so that positive Qi may gather in the surrounding area. Ideally, we are looking for the "armchair" placement, but it may be hard to find this in nature. In its absence, an artificial armchair placement can be created by planning the design of the buildings on the lot, as well as the placement of trees and the use of the existing natural environment.

It is not advisable to build houses immediately adjacent to or at the bottom of a mountain. The quality of Qi descending down a hillside is very Yin (with a downward Qi movement, such as in the T'ai Qi symbol) and is most intense at the bottom of the mountain where, ultimately, it gathers in full strength. Therefore, such a site would be ideal for a grave, not for a Yang home. Traditionally, such a location is known to bring on mysterious illnesses and a slow decline in health. Ideally, a building should be placed farther away from a mountainside, leaving at least a deeper backyard in between.

When designing a new building, it is preferable to take into account all of the features of the natural environment that fit the existing landscape harmoniously as much as possible. The ideal land on which to start new construction is well leveled and possibly provides a softly shaped hill or mountain at the rear (Vienna, AT).

Case Study: Julie

This personal story of tragic consequence illustrates the importance of land elevation and juxtaposition as important factors in Feng Shui design.

In the late fifties, Julie and her husband acquired a piece of property in the San Fernando Valley along the Hollywood Hills. Although they designed their house on level ground, the back of it lay immediately adjacent to the hillside. After a few years, Julie's husband developed a severe health problem related to a scarcity in the production of white cells. His immune system became so weakened that he contracted many illnesses in succession, from simple colds to pneumonia.

Julie consulted doctors from all over the world, but the cause of her husband's illness could not be found. Although high-dose vitamin injections invigorated his system, they did not produce any long lasting effect. Julie persevered for thirteen years, trying to

Plots of land that are not level are considered unfavorable for new construction. In this case it is advisable to level the land, perhaps with the help of retaining walls, to create a more favorable site (Sacramento, CA)

find a cure for her husband's illness. After a long period of debilitation, he died, and the cause of his death remains unknown. From the point of view of Feng Shui, it is clear that the negative Qi descending down the hillside immediately adjacent to Julie's home may have had a profound impact on her husband's health.

More on Land Elevation

A house built below grade, or on a level lower than the street elevation, receives descending Qi, or Yin Qi. A building constructed in this manner receives energy that is not supportive for the Yang physiology of living people, possibly contributing to the deterioration of their health and or their finances. Ideally, the ground should be raised to street level or a bit higher before commencing the construction of a building. If the lot is sizable enough, the street traffic is not too heavy, and there is an open view on the side opposite the street, the house can be oriented to face the rear view so that the high level of the street would be behind the building, serving partially as a supporting "tortoise." This suggestion should be evaluated on a case-by-case basis as it relates to the entire surrounding environment and to the size and shape of the lot.

A house built below grade (below street level) suffers from the oppression of the Yin Qi generated around the road. It is always preferable to build houses at street level or slightly higher.

A house built on the edge of a cliff can cause instability and anxiety in its inhabitants because of the sudden drop of Qi flow in the environment. A flat area between the building and the drop is preferable to allow Qi to gather around the building. Ideally, the building should be located as far away from the cliff as possible, utilizing trees and plants to soften the effects of the drop and to retain beneficial Qi around the building.

A house built on posts typically causes stomach problems, emotional instability, and financial loss because of the lack of a solid and homogeneous foundation to support the household although plants and bushes that can be planted underneath to stop the Qi movement and create more stability. A basement can be created with outside walls to fill the space between the posts all the way around. This situation is more severe if the ground underneath it is not leveled or if the house is standing over water. This is a difficult situation to correct because of the combination of unfavorable features. In fact, the water's humidity and movement aggravates the instability of the building's Qi even more.

A house hanging from the side of a hill suffers from Qi depletion and lacks supportive energy for its occupants.

A house that is built on a hillside, especially on a severe slope, cannot gather Qi from its surroundings. This results in a depletion of the positive energy and it can cause severe financial instability and loss. Bushes and trees around the building can help hold positive Qi; however, I would not suggest this type of land for a building purchase. When building from scratch, leveling the ground and adding retaining walls is suggested prior to beginning the construction of the house.

Buildings constructed on hilltops, along the sides of hills, or on posts have difficulty in retaining life-force energy and have the potential for creating instability in the well-being and finances of the building's occupants.

Case Study: Andy

After looking for the ideal house for many years, Andy believed that his dream was finally imminent: he found a two-story, three-bedroom home overlooking a lake at a fantastically low price for the location. During the long drive to the property, I advised Andy that simply knowing the previous owners' experience with the house could give him some indication of the Feng Shui qualities of the building.

During the review of the property, I noticed at least four Feng Shui challenges: the house was not only built on a hillside, but posts supported the front part, and the main entrance was located below grade and on the outside blade of a curve in the road. It appeared to me not to be the most desirable place to live. I tried to explain to Andy that this house was likely to cause him major financial loss, but his enthusiasm for the house was overwhelming. I suggested that he ask the real estate agent about the previous owners and their reasons for moving out.

Upon investigation, he found that the two previous pairs of owners went bankrupt, both within a year of buying the house, and had to foreclose, which was why the house was on the market at such a low price. Wisely, Andy decided to put his dream on hold for awhile, waiting for a better opportunity to invest his savings. Several months later, while going over a local real estate journal, I found the same house still on the market. Despite its low price, the property was not appealing enough on an energy level to attract people to invest in it.

Lot Size, Shape, and Lot-to-Building Ratio

The shape and size of a lot have a considerable effect on the flow of Qi around a building.

Below are some examples of lot-to-building ratios that can serve as overall proportion guidelines when in the pre-purchase selection phase. On a case-by-case analysis, a Feng Shui expert may consider exceptions to these ratios.

To have good Feng Shui qualities, a lot should have a regular shape. Irregularly shaped lots should be evaluated on a case-by-case base.

The most desirable lot shape is square or slightly rectangular. The four-sided shape allows for the maximum and most consistent flow of Qi from the surrounding property, which will benefit the entire building.

A building should be designed to be proportionate in size to the lot on which it is situated. The square-footage of a one-story building should not be more than one-fourth its lot size. This ratio enables a consistent flow of Qi from the surrounding environment to "feed the building." This ratio refers to regularly shaped lots. The more irregular the lot, the bigger the ratio should be.

For a building of two stories or more, the distance from adjacent buildings should allow for abundant sunlight and avoid the so-called "canyon shade" effect. Unfortunately, this condition may be difficult to satisfy in an urban environment, where land is scarce and costly, and every square foot is exploited.

If the lot has a trapezoid shape, it is preferable that the back side be larger than the front. As a large bottle with a small opening holds liquid well and disperses it slowly, a lot with a large back and smaller front will retain Qi better.

Thus, a home built on such a lot, will attract more prosperity than a house on a lot whose front is larger than its back. Like a vase with a large mouth, such a lot might attract a greater Qi flow, but it will tend to lose it as well. In this case the proportion between building and lot should be at least 1 to 6, and plants and bushes may be used to correct the irregularity.

Triangular-shaped lots are considered inauspicious because they do not have either a straight back or a straight facade. Qi cannot flow harmoniously into such awkward shapes, nor can it be gathered within the buildings. The only exception is when the lot's dimensions are considerably bigger then the building on it. Utilizing trees and a tailored landscape design can give the lot a more regular shape and thus contribute to a more favorable flow of Qi. The ratio must be at least one-eighth or higher.

Small lots with irregular shapes are never beneficial, as the Qi flow is irregular and can easily stagnate or deplete erratically. Although similar to the above case, if the lot size allows for it, landscaping may correct the problem. For example, trees and bushes can be used to correct overextended corners to give a more regular shape to the lot and ensure a more balanced and consistent flow of Qi. However, the building that can be accommodated on such a small lot should consequently be small, maintaining a ratio of one-sixth to one-eighth or more.

Feng Shui in Wind and Water Patterns

Feng = Wind

Wind, as *feng*, is very important when considering location. Soft breezes are beneficial to carry the Qi, but strong winds break it and blow it away, preventing the house from receiving its benefit.

When a building is exposed to strong wind, trees may be planted as a buffer between the wind and the building to protect it. This correction is most effective on open, flat land where there are no mountains. In general, trees help to hold Qi around the building, and they can be used at the back or on the sides to create armchair positioning.

A house built on top of a mountain or on the ridge of a hill may have difficulty in retaining Qi because of too much wind exposure. Trees are not as effective in this circumstance because of the instability of strong Qi movement as it follows an ascending and descending pattern along the mountain. It is preferable to build a home in a more protected environment because if other buildings surround it, they may provide stronger protection and support than trees.

Shui = Water

Water, as *shui*, is the other important element and is associated with abundance and prosperity. In its primal state, it is always clean and flowing gently. These qualities make it productive. Water can also create negative situations, and therefore it is important to design with a clear understanding of water's many dynamics.

A house location on the inside curve of a stream is considered the best choice. However, there may be some exceptions to this circumstance. Only a well-trained master can recognize when it is appropriate to place water at the rear of a building.

A location close to a stream of rushing water is not so advisable, as it can drain away the Qi, adversely affecting health and prosperity. If there are no other possibilities, place a line of trees and bushes between the building and the stream to create a separation and stabilize the Qi around the building.

Living close to a large body of water can also be very positive. However, if the location is too close to a lake or sea, the effect can be overwhelming and it can create Water *Sha* (see following chapters), turning the Yang effects of water into Yin effects. Typical Yin effects of water are excessive humidity, mold, rot, and unpleasant odors.

Houses built above a waterfall or a stream of water are highly undesirable because this position can cause instability in the grounding of the building on account of the water's movement. Moreover, this placement creates a high level of humidity and Yin Qi, particularly in winter, possibly making the occupants ill.

Urban Environments and Manmade Structures

In ancient times, Feng Shui was reserved principally for designing palaces for the Chinese emperors, aristocrats, and noblemen. It was seldom that commoners benefited from this philosophy of design. In a modern, hectic, and compact city like Hong Kong, however, no structure is built without the advice and guidance of a Feng Shui master, who is generally compensated very generously for his or her services. In the US, Australia, and Europe, these benefits are now sought out more and more frequently.

Buildings as Mountains

In urban areas, where mountains are not often part of the landscape, a building can be supported by adjacent buildings. Here are some helpful guidelines:

The building under consideration should generally be as tall as or slightly shorter than the one behind it, but not too much; otherwise its rear neighbor will oppress it.

The buildings on the sides should be of the same height or slightly shorter, but not much shorter, or the upper floors of the building may be exposed to the elements and not protected enough.

In an urban environment, buildings can have the same impact as mountains. Particularly in the downtown regions of big cities, it is preferable to live and work in areas where the buildings are approximately the same height, as they are more likely to support and protect each other (Chicago, IL).

A larger building that greatly overshadows a smaller one will cause a sense of oppression and could create a lack of confidence in the smaller building's occupants.

Conversely, a taller building surrounded by short buildings will be buffeted by the wind in every direction and this will bring instability to its occupants. As a general rule, buildings close to each other should be more or less the same height. The principal idea behind this configuration is that in a building that has no protection, the Qi will tend to be blown away by the wind. Thus, neighboring buildings of proportionate height and distance help support each other, protecting one another from the wind and sheltering the surrounding beneficial Qi.

The "wind-tunnel effect" between high-rise buildings can be very destructive and difficult to counteract. It is advisable, therefore, to seriously consider wind patterns before choosing an apartment or a commercial building. In particular, it may be wise to reject

A short building located among much taller buildings could suffer from pressure and oppression of its Qi, making it undesirable from a Feng Shui perspective (Chicago, IL).

A single tall building among lower buildings will be unprotected, and the wind will disperse its Qi, making it undesirable from the standpoint of Feng Shui.

buildings that are wedged tightly between other buildings, or exposed apartments that are located on the upper floors of tall buildings where the surrounding buildings are shorter.

Ground floor garages are highly contrary to good Feng Shui. Not only will the building not be grounded, but the movement of cars entering and exiting and the vibration produced under the living floors will also make the overall Qi of the building highly unstable.

Roads as Water Courses

As previously mentioned, in an urban milieu where there are no mountains or rivers, streets serve as Qi carriers, and their positions can

The wind tunnel effect created among tall buildings in an urban environment is considered unfavorable for a building located at the receiving end. The building will be assaulted by a very strong Qi that may be the cause of financial or personal losses (Chicago, IL).

either be very beneficial or negative, as the following situations illustrate:

A house sitting on the inside curve of a road will bring its occupants health, wealth, and career advancement. Conversely, houses sitting on the outside blade of a curve can bring poverty, sickness, and bad luck to its occupants. In this case, bushes and plants can be used to buffer the intense Sha Qi from the street.

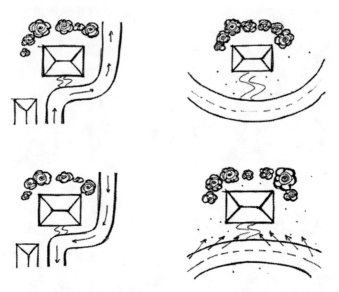

The shape and the direction of a road can relate to the adjacent houses in a favorable or unfavorable manner and it should be planned accordingly.

Houses with roads pointing toward them at a T or Y intersection are generally not favorable and can bring severe disabilities. In a few exceptional cases, such a location can bring extraordinary wealth, but only a thorough mastery of Feng Shui would enable the individual to tell the difference. Again, plants and bushes can be used to buffer the assault of intense Qi.

A building with streets running along two opposite sides may cause sleep disorders, low productivity, and mental difficulties in school or at work. If the lot is large enough, plants can be placed along the streets, between them and the building, to soften this destabilizing effect.

A house with a one-way street along either side of its entrance can be either very favorable or unfavorable regarding wealth. If the direction of the traffic is toward the front of the house, the Qi tends to bring prosperity; if it is heading away from the house, the Qi tends to carry abundance away. However, in most cases, it is highly preferable to have a road softly curving around the property.

Corner buildings are exposed to the unstable Qi activity of the intersection, which often pulls and pushes in different direction. This can cause instability in the Qi of the corner house and in the life of its occupants.

The same building after implementing Feng Shui corrections: with extensive use of rose bushes along the outer corner, the strong Qi from the street has been buffered. The use of curtains to screen the large windows helps to contain the Qi in the house and screen the excessive Yang energy from the outside.

In an urban environment, streets and streams have similar characteristics. Freeway traffic, however, generates strong Qi activity, and this is often more a Sha Qi (polluted energy) then a Sheng Qi (healthy energy). It is preferable not to live or work in a building adjacent to a freeway, especially at a lower level (El Segundo, CA).

The intense Qi movement generated by freeway traffic brings an enormous amount of Yin Qi (or Sha) to houses residing below or alongside. A location on the outer blade of a freeway curve makes a building especially prone to the negative effects of this Yin Qi.

A driveway leading to a building should contribute to activating favorable Qi in that area without assaulting the building with a straight, aggressive path.

The driveway of a house should also be planned so as to direct Qi toward the building in a favorable manner. In a straight path, pointing to the entry door, it will funnel the Qi too strongly against the building (Leesburg, VA).

A curving driveway leading to a garage can become very favorable in directing the Qi to activate that part of the building, especially if a positive entrance is located in the same area (Las Vegas, NV).

Chapter 6

LANDSCAPE DESIGN AND GARDEN ARRANGEMENT

The landscape design surrounding a building is directly related to the building's energy and layout. Its function should be to support the building's existing energy.

As previously discussed, a building should leave some breathing room for Qi to flow in the surrounding area; it should not occupy the entire lot. Obviously, this condition is easier to fulfill in the countryside, whereas the inherent space limitations of a city make it more difficult.

Garden Purpose and Style

The purpose of a garden is primarily to help balance the energy of the building and to create a favorable interaction between the interior and the exterior. Whatever style feels comfortable to you is the style you should choose. Appealing to your natural tastes and inclinations constitutes a point of advantage in your personal Feng Shui.

It is commonly believed that a Chinese-style garden is automatically "good Feng Shui." This is not necessarily so. This style may be just as good or bad as any other. If you like this style, then choose it; but if you don't, you need not feel guilty about choosing a different one because, as long as it follows the recommendations outlined in this book or those of a Traditional Feng Shui expert, it is going to be favorable.

Classical styles, while ornate and majestic, may also cause irregular Qi flow. For example, the highly refined Italian gardens may be too rigid with their straight and uniformly designed patterns, while an English romantic garden may attract Yin energy because of the irregular levels of the land. Although such gardens may be appropriate for an Italian villa or an English Tudor manor, as far as design is concerned, they would probably not be appropriate for most other homes.

Landscape Design Considerations

When considering landscaping and gardens, the design principal to keep in mind is the harmony between the house and its surrounding landscape in order to enable the maximum flow of positive Qi. The proper garden size and the help of an expert can contribute immensely to the beauty of the site. There are no fixed rules with respect to types of plant, colors, or the shape of the leaves since the energy outside of the building changes often and is much more flexible than the interior energy.

Landscape layout designers should be most aware of external environment corrections, such as establishing a smooth flow of visible Qi around the building and buffering any Sha energy (see nest chapter). The basic rules for good Feng Shui in a garden are to support the building's energy. This includes creating some "armchair" protection and support, and positioning water elements and other features such as a rock garden, pagoda, or gazebo, that may be necessary on a case-by-case analysis.

Personally, I'd rather dedicate an area in front of the house to a lawn with some plants and trees, if lot size permits, so that the building does not sit so immediately exposed to the street. This is traditionally referred to as *Ming Tong*.

I also like to assign some garden area in the backyard at a reasonable distance from neighboring homes. As a result, the backyard becomes more private and peaceful, suitable for family gatherings, children's play, and quiet time to recharge one's batteries after work.

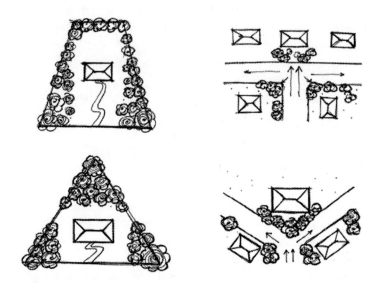

Trees and plants can be used for a variety of purposes during landscape design. This picture shows how to correct an irregularly shaped lot and how to screen houses from an unfavorable assault of Sha Qi when adjacent to a T—or Y-shaped intersection.

Garden "No-Nos"

A chaotic and disorderly garden, with dying vegetation or overgrown plants, creates feelings of confusion and turmoil and should be avoided. Conversely, well-tended gardens increase the flow and gathering of Qi and make the surrounding area positive as well.

It is preferable to have a well-leveled site rather than one with bumps and holes, as these create small pockets of stagnating Yin Qi that will spoil the quality of the entire site.

Trees and Plants

Correcting Lot Shape and Creating the Armchair

As previously discussed, trees and plants are the best corrections for sites with irregular shapes. They create the favorable armchair

The use of bamboo trees to screen a house from the Qi assault of an X-shaped intersection has transformed the area adjacent to the house into a quiet garden (Hollywood Hills, CA). Gene Ogami photography.

placement to support the structure, correct an off-angle corner and create more harmony in the flow of Qi of the entire garden. They can also be used in the back or on the sides to substitute a "mountain" arrangement or an adjacent building.

Protection from Inauspicious Sha

Trees and bushes are also an excellent way to screen your property from inauspicious urban environmental features or negative Qi (Sha).

For example, someone with a house that faces a T-shaped intersection, with a road pointing toward the building, can use bushes or a hedge as protection from the intense Qi directed toward it.

A harsh corner from an adjacent building pointing toward yours, especially if facing the entrance or a bedroom, should be screened as much as possible.

Planning Ahead

If gardens are located near the house, they can create a cool and fresh environment. However, in selecting plants for the garden, it is also important to consider the sun exposure. Tall plants that bring shade and coolness (Yin) will balance the stronger sun (Yang) of a southern exposure. Smaller plants that do not mask the weaker sunlight of a northern exposure will allow the natural light from the northeast and northwest to nourish the house. However, large plants in a garden with a northern exposure can have an unfavorable effect on the Qi flow of a building and they can create excessive Yin Qi, which could cause fungus and mold.

Overgrown plants can overwhelm a building and produce a sense of insecurity and disorder for the residents. Thus, it is important when selecting trees, to consider their future growth so they don't end up suffocating the house. Sometimes, overgrown roots can also damage the plumbing and wiring.

When planting, be aware of the future growth of each plant. There is no point in planting an oak tree right next to the entry door because it will eventually grow so high that you may either have to remove it or relocate it. Plant it farther away from the building so that you can still enjoy the view from the window and it where it will not become an impediment in the future.

Unfavorable Landscape Conditions

If situated too close to a building, plants absorb air and sunlight that would otherwise nourish a house, causing drainage of Qi. A dark environment is the first sign of stagnating Qi and it is also considered very Yin. It prevents the house from receiving sunlight, causing excess humidity in the environment and depression and sadness in the occupants, as well as increasing the possibility of serious illness. When there are large plants close to a building, it is important, to have them trimmed regularly to avoid overgrowth that may reduce light and air flow.

When trees and plants grow too close to a house, they absorb the life-force energy while preventing the sun's radiation from positively energizing the building. If numerous, they may cause a depletion of the building's Qi that can affect the occupants unfavorably.

Good Feng Shui means having healthy, well trimmed, good looking plants around us. Dying plants absorb higher quantities of healthy Qi. They should either be brought back to health or removed.

Fountains and Pools

Water is a purifying element that can both enhance our garden and landscape design and attract prosperity. To be around water makes us feel good because it releases negative ions, which are extremely beneficial. Moreover, the sounds of a brook or a waterfall are very soothing.

Water and Qi

Good Qi is preserved by fresh, clean, moving water. Stagnant and putrid water brings the opposite effect: Sha, often in the form of bad luck and financial problems.

Clean, flowing water has the capacity to absorb, energize, and then release healthy Qi into an environment. Softly shaped pools and ponds are beneficial, as they create a harmonious flow of water (Hollywood Hills, CA). Gene Ogami photography.

To be effective, water should move and flow, but at the same time it should be contained at the bottom. In this case, water goes underground for recycling, thereby causing a dispersion of Qi.

Water features should have movement that allows the water to flow in the open air, increasing the Qi circulation. However, the majority of water should gather at the bottom in a basin-type container and create a sense and feeling of mass. When movement exists without any containment, the benefits will be lost. For example, water sprinklers, no matter how abundant the amount of water they generate, are not as effective as a proper water remedy.

Water placement in a garden is also related to a building's energy and it can help correct one or more existing imbalances within the building. Only a well-trained expert can determine the specific characteristics a water feature should have and in which area it will be most effective.

An infinity pool creates a beautiful effect of endlessness, but it also causes water to flow away from the building without any boundaries or containment. When overlooking a large, open space, it may become a vehicle for Qi depletion.

Shape and Size of Water Features

The shape of a pond or a swimming pool must be integrated as much as possible with the design of the building and the landscape. For example, an aggressive design that contrasts with a soft, curvy landscape can cause discomfort and produce visual disturbance. Remember, beauty and harmony are the main goals of Feng Shui and should be pursued in every aspect of design.

A large water feature shouldn't be placed too close to a building, otherwise its effects may be overwhelming causing Yin Qi. An infinity-pool at the edge of a cliff may create a beautiful feeling of openness. However, this will not contribute to holding the Qi around the building; it will dissipate it through the falling water.

A Cautionary Note

Given all the positive attributes of water, proper location is crucial. Instead of creating wealth, improper placement of a beautiful

The strength of the water element can be enhanced with the use of metal elements. In this case, the fixtures are made of copper, which strengthens the water's energy as it flows through them.

koi pond or of a cascading waterfall and fountain or a huge swimming pool might drain one's finances.

In particular, no water feature should have been located in the western region of a garden until the year 2004. That direction had received the best "prosperity Qi" during that twenty year cycle (1984-2003), and it was associated with the metal element (Dui trigram). According to the cycle of the Five Elements, placing water in this direction would have drained the metal energy and thus the prosperity energy as well.

Garden Timing

Choosing the right time for gardening is essential. Because of the different energy cycles occurring every year, there is always a section of the garden where construction or digging should be avoided. This area changes from year to year.

February 5th through the following February 4th constitutes the Feng Shui year, according to the Chinese solar calendar. This calendar is entirely based on the Earth's rotation around the sun and the consequent cycle of seasons and Earth-related changes.

Each year, one portion of the garden is ruled by very strong Earth energy, which is not conducive to our well-being and good fortune in general. Digging disturbs the energy, creates Earth Sha and spreads it throughout the property. As a result, accidents are more likely to occur, and if the excavation is considerable, the whole house can be adversely affected. The best way to prevent this situation is to postpone gardening in that area until the following year. If you have begun digging already, placing metal, like wire mesh or a statue or, when appropriate, metal wind chimes between your house and the affected area, will offset the negative influences released by the digging. According to the Five Elements Theory, metal reduces Earth energy in a gentle, harmonious way.

Weak Areas to Avoid

Below is a list of garden areas where digging should be avoided, according to the year. As energy moves in cycles and once the directions have come full circle, start the cycle over from the beginning. Remember that these directions refer to the position of the magnetic north, and therefore in order to properly identify them it advisable to use a compass.

Current Year	Garden Section
2003	Southeast Section
2004	Center Section
2005	Northwest Section
2006	West Section
2007	Northeast Section
2008	South Section
2009	North Section
2010	Southwest Section
2011	East Section
2012	SouthEast Section
2013	Center Section

Table 3. Areas where digging should be avoided, according to the year

Chapter 7

SHA VS. QI: DANGEROUS FEATURES TO AVOID

Just as it is crucial to know and attune ourselves to the positive life force called Qi, it is equally imperative to identify and avoid or correct its negative counterpart, called Sha. Qi is mostly positive and beneficial and can be weak or strong. Sha, however, is "polluted energy" that brings deterioration to our health and well-being. Excessively strong Qi can also become unhealthy, and turn into Sha. Stagnant, obstructed Qi that doesn't flow properly, spoils, and decays, thus becoming polluted, creates Sha.

How do we identify Sha in our environment?

Sha and the Five Elements

The first kind of Sha relates to the Five Elements. It is caused by environmental features that capture an excess of Qi belonging to one of the elements and causes a Qi imbalance in the surroundings. Such features should be corrected, and their imbalance softened or released, allowing harmony and balance to be restored. Below is a discussion of the most common environmental features that produce Sha according to the Five Elements:

Fire Sha

Fire Sha is caused mostly by manmade sources of electromagnetism, such as appliances, computers and electrical posts. This is extremely difficult for nature to counteract, since the electromagnetic waves emitted from these manmade sources are extraordinarily strong. These devices increase the intensity of the fire energy in the environment, causing potential problems to human physiology by conflicting with the more subtle, natural energy field of the body.

In general, sources of manmade electromagnetism in the bedroom, such as a TV, computer or electrical clock, are not advisable. The bedroom is the place where we rest and rejuvenate, while the presence of strong manmade electromagnetic fields have the opposite effect.

Large power lines create extremely severe Fire Sha that can potentially cause serious illnesses. Studies conducted in Europe show a strong connection between the magnetic field created by large power lines and leukemia, cancer, and modifications of the genetic code. Therefore, living close to power lines should be avoided as much as possible.

Although smaller electric poles may be acceptable, the proximity to transformers (big round gray boxes hanging from the poles) should be avoided. It is particularly unfavorable if the pole holding the transformer is adjacent to the bedroom or any other area where much time is spent.

If the proximity to sources of Fire Sha is unavoidable, you can introduce earth elements to absorb and attenuate their unfavorable effects. For example, you can install rocks, tiles, clay statues, and pottery in the interior of the house and a rock garden or a terra cotta tile patio outdoors. Plants and bushes are also effective in reducing the intensity of outdoor Fire Sha because of their capacity to counteract the magnetic field generated by electricity. The amount of earth element has to be proportional to the size of the magnetic field. If it is overwhelmingly large, the remedy may not be sufficient.

Metal Sha

Metal Sha is by far the most dangerous Sha Qi that one could encounter in our environment. Caused by sharp, edgy corners

Although electrical fixtures are not as critical as power lines, it is preferable not to be too close to transformer boxes.

pointing towards a house, Metal Sha is often referred to as "poisoned arrow" or "pointed arrows" for its strength and sharpness. I think of it as a powerful, sharp energy similar to a blade.

If the corners are small and located in the interior, the effects are usually minor, but if the corners have a considerable dimension and are located at a close distance outside the house, the effects can be severe.

Living in a building facing a pointed roof or a pointed building or any other pointed structure is not advisable. If the magnetic field of the house is not strong and balanced, the pointed structure facing it can bring fatalities to the occupants, especially when negative earth energy is located in the pointed area. According to the classics, for example, if a pointed corner faces a Qian (northwest) quadrant, it will cause problems in the head, if it faces a Li (south) quadrant it can cause eye maladies; and if it faces a Kan (north) quadrant, it can cause kidney problems, etc.

The most effective way to reduce Metal Sha is to place trees, bushes, and plants between your home and the source of Sha. Vegetation absorbs and softens the effects of the "pointed arrow."

A fountain or any other water source can also be used, since water reduces metal according to the Five Elements Theory. Water can easily be introduced into a garden, especially if it surrounds the building. Make sure, however, that the water is clean and always moving.

Earth Sha

In the "time-space" Xuan Kong school (which uses the Flying Stars technique), Earth Sha is often related to time cycles. Earth Sha deals with negative energy that is caused by disturbing the soil and altering its natural dynamics.

Based on the year (utilizing information gathered according to the Table 3 in the previous chapter), digging in negative-energy areas can have serious consequences on the well being of the entire household.

Moreover, excavated earth, especially if left in unsightly piles on property for prolonged periods, can be particularly unpleasant and even dangerous.

Sharp, angular corners are considered Metal Sha, a very powerful inauspicious feature. In this picture the tall building with a pointed roof on the right and the rhomboid building on the left can both be considered sources of Metal Sha. Living or working in a building directly exposed to such a strong feature can cause financial or personal problems (Chicago, IL).

This also relates to geopathic stress, studied extensively in Europe by Celtic geomancers and geobiologists. It involves primarily natural soil gases and radiations unfavorable for the human physiology.

Wood Sha

An excessive amount of tall trees too close to a building absorbs all of the Qi flow, thereby suffocating the inhabitants and creating feelings of depression and heaviness.

A tall tree directly aligned with the entry door splits the Qi flow and pre-vents it from entering the house. If the tree has exceptionally large dimen-sions, its size will overpower the house, creating a lack of confidence and insecurity in the occupants.

Dying plants also deplete the environment of healthy Qi. This is more critical inside a building then outside; however, dead trees close to a building should be removed immediately.

Trees placed right in front of the entrance create Sha because they absorb and break the natural Qi that flows towards the entrance, depriving the building of receiving its sustenance.

Unsightly posts such as telephone poles, traffic signs, and construction placards or other markers too close to an entrance are also forms of Wood Sha. These objects cause the Qi to break its flow, making it weaker.

Buildings overlooking a large ravine or forest of sizable trees can be very unstable because of the impact that these large masses of trees can have on a building's energy. With few exceptions that only a skilled Feng Shui expert can recognize, it is rather preferable to have this large number of trees in the back or on the sides, rather than in the front.

Water Sha

Living close to water is very pleasant and undoubtedly conducive to health. However, if the water is dirty, stagnant, or putrid, this can pose a real health hazard.

Straight, rigid channels of rushing water, even if pure, should also be avoided, as they move Qi too quickly and drain it away from a building, causing ripples of chaotic Qi around the property.

Urban corollaries, such as freeways and highly traveled boulevards and streets, are also comparable forms of Water Sha.

Underground streams cause excessive moisture to permeate the Qi radiating up from the earth. This excessive humidity creates a Yin condition that is not favorable for a Yang house and can aggravate other negative conditions.

Sha and the Five Senses

Any feature of our surroundings that is jarring to our five senses is considered a source of Sha. The effects on human physiology can be subtle, but constant exposure can diminish our strength day by day. In time, we may think that we have successfully adjusted to the unfavorable energy, but in reality, our senses and physiology have weakened so that we are no longer capable of responding to the danger. The five types of Sha related to our senses are sight, smell, sound, touch, and taste.

The only way to adjust the Sha that is directed at our five senses is to eliminate the source of uncomfortable feelings and transform it into something beautiful and satisfying. When moving to a new home or office, if right from the start we realize that some things bother us, we must address and correct the sources of our discomfort as soon as possible, before we get used to them and are no longer capable of recognizing or responding to the problems.

Sight Sha

Sight Sha is the most common of the five senses and it occurs with any disturbing visual image around the building.

133

A house close to a gravesite is not favorable. The excessive Yin Qi generated by the compound of burials is highly toxic to the Yang nature of living people. This exposure will cause sadness and depression over time.

Dirty streets, a rundown building, a misshapen garden where plants grow chaotically, or simply an aggressive design or colors that don't match the surrounding neighborhood are all manifestations of Sight Sha.

Within our homes, Sight Sha can arise if furniture is mismatched or colors do not match each other or when art objects, no matter their cost, are not aesthetically pleasing to the eye.

A house that overlooks a burial ground is not advisable, as it brings pessimism and sadness. Nor is it advisable to locate a building on top of an old cemetery or burial site. The presence of very intense Yin Qi from Yin houses (burials) works against the well-being of the living.

Smell Sha

Smell Sha is frequently the most overlooked form of Sha. Too often do we not pay attention to its powerful, destructive effects. The air we breathe brings pure life-force energy into the body, so when the air around us is polluted, it can damage our health severely.

Houses that have been closed for a long time or that have humidity problems often retain a stuffy and moldy atmosphere deep inside that is totally inimical to good health. Of course, this situation is not resolved simply because we get used to it and forget how clean air smells and feels and how it nourishes us.

A house that overlooks a dumpsite or that is built on top of a former dumpsite should definitely be avoided. The disturbing view, unpleasant smell, and methane gas produced by the garbage underneath it is enough to pollute both the air and the Qi, making the overall environment unsuitable and unhealthy.

Every form of pollution generated by industry or by automobiles introduces toxins into the system, whether we realize it or not. The pervasion of Smell Sha in big cities can incapacitate our ability to identify smells. In children, it can contribute to a variety of breathing disorders such as allergies, asthma, and sinusitis.

The only way to correct Smell Sha is to eliminate its source or move to a less polluted area or house, ideally before medical conditions become chronic and irreversible.

Sound Sha

Sound Sha is a common cause of disturbance, especially in big cities, though it can also be present in rural areas.

Constant background noise caused by street traffic, airports, noisy neighbors, or sirens and alarms is becoming more and more disturbing to the human physiology and is a primary cause of stress.

Houses built close to a police station, fire station, or hospital do not assure a quiet environment for their inhabitants. The constant state of emergency and noise can be disturbing and unsettling to nearby residents.

Living in big cities, we seem to adapt to noise. It is not until we return from a few quiet days in the country that we realize how deleterious Sound Sha can be to our health. We find it more difficult to fall asleep, and we become more irritable or edgy upon awakening.

Again, the only way to recover from the negative effects of Sound Sha is to eliminate as much of the source of noise as possible. To counteract Sound Sha, place trees and bushes around the building to buffer the noise. Insulate your home with soundproofing materials, or install water fixtures such as cascading fountains to produce a mellifluous sound that will help mask the noise. If the problem persists, consider moving to a more placid location.

Touch Sha

Touch Sha is mostly related to interior design and the selection of materials. The consistency, texture, and finishing of items in and around our homes may bring feelings of comfort or discomfort. These are the kinds of things that immediately trigger a reaction in us when touched by our hands or bodies. Examples of Touch Sha elements are:

- sticky surfaces
- a cold marble table top
- cold tile or stone flooring
- a rough comforter
- sharp-angled furniture

If exposed to such elements for a long time, we undermine our sense of ease and comfort and compromise the full enjoyment of being at home.

Conclusions Regarding Selecting a Site

After all of these considerations, you may by now have a clearer picture of what to look for and what to avoid in the exterior environment of your property. If, after determining all possible changes and corrections, you discover that a site is still fifty percent (or more) undesirable, it may be time to consider passing on it. Without regrets and with the confidence of now knowing more about what you are looking for, search for something better.

If you are in the process of building from scratch, you have to consider that the outside environment is the most difficult to correct because its effects are large and involve the entire site. This shouldn't be underestimated. No mirror, crystal ball or wind chime can fix that. It shouldn't be taken lightly, especially when choosing a lot to acquire. This could be a strong point of advantage to capitalize on or a point of disadvantage that may result in a poor building overall.

In some cases, a Traditional Feng Shui expert may advise on a landscape layout that is different from what we have discussed so far. This due to specific characteristics of a building (or a building to be) that needs exceptional exterior environmental features to balance its internal energy. Such exceptions will be best evaluated under strict supervision of a Traditional Feng Shui expert.

Chapter 8

DESIGNING INTERIORS

The design features of a building are often appreciated for their aesthetics alone. Some buildings, such as landmark skyscrapers are striking examples of fine contemporary architectural design and others, such as an ancient villa in an Italian countryside, may be considered a masterpiece of the past. According to Feng Shui, beauty and proportion in design are certainly important, since anything unpleasant to the sight becomes a form of Sha.

The physical appearance of a building is important only to the extent that it is combined with design features that enhance the well-being of its inhabitants. A building composed of fashionable or trendy aesthetic features alone, but devoid of a healthy and harmonious environment, is like a well-decorated corpse; it may be pleasing to the eye, but its life-sustaining energy is absent.

If a building has good natural energy, the job of a good designer would be to enhance it effectively. Typically, the front part of a house, where the main entrance is located, would be considered the face, which is the most Yang area; the center is the heart; and the bedrooms and bathrooms located at the back are more Yin in nature. When working with a Feng Shui architect in designing a building, you may at times receive suggestions that vary from this simple scheme. These suggestions are generally based on the occupants' dates of birth, the building's invisible energy distribution and power areas, and its interaction with the outside environment and location.

Conditions for a Desirable Building

To enhance the well-being of a building's inhabitants, the design should allow for a smooth flow of Qi through its interior. Just as we use acupuncture to remove obstacles to good Qi flow through the meridians (energy pathways) of our bodies, so should we use Feng Shui to open the flow of obstructed Qi in the interior of a building.

Often, when reviewing the floor plan of a new building or of a remodeling project, I can identify design conditions that are more desirable and recommend making corrections while the design is still on paper.

For good interior architecture in Feng Shui terms, a desirable building should consist of the following:

- A desirable shape
- A good flow of Qi inside each room and from room to room (floor plan/layout)
- A well-designed interior and exterior (architectural features)
- A good match between the energy of the building, the color palette, and the materials
- A good balance of light and shade
- A favorable entrance location and design
- A favorable bedroom location and design

While good-looking designs can be achieved with the work of skilled architects and interior designers, this is usually not the case with respect to a favorable building shape or a floor plan that ensures a smooth flow of Qi through the interior.

In existing buildings, these characteristics are more difficult to change or may require extensive structural remodeling. It is therefore advisable to address them as carefully as possible when planning the original design.

Conditions to Avoid

The following are several negative conditions to avoid or eliminate in a building:

- Floor plan design that can cause stagnation, which can create "spoiled" Qi
- Design features that obstruct the flow of Qi through the interior of a building
- Interior Sha, which occurs when Qi flows too heavily in one direction
- Strong drafts, which blow away Qi (remember, *feng* means wind, which either carries Qi if it moves at a smooth and gentle pace or depletes and disperses Qi if it moves too fast.)
- Any imbalance or excess of Yin or Yang

Each of the situations described above modifies and ultimately affects the proper supply and quality of Qi in the building's interior. Our "healthy Qi" becomes spoiled (Sha) and either decays due to stagnation, or depletes due to improper wind circulation. When we interact with stagnant or void Qi, we may not experience the negative effects immediately, but in the long run the process may take its tole on our personal Qi.

Over the years, I have become very sensitive to these situations. At times, when analyzing existing buildings where an unfavorable situation is present, I may ask clients to experience it briefly in person under my supervision. During our conference, I then explain to them why they felt the way they did and what it is that they were experiencing. Not only do they often become more aware of how much a building's environment affects them, but they also soon realize how certain areas that have better Feng Shui are physically more comfortable than those with unfavorable negative Feng Shui qualities.

My personal experience is that, after a few weeks of living in an environment with these kinds of problems, we can feel progressively more tired without really being able to pinpoint why. In the beginning, we try subconsciously to force our bodies to comply with the unfavorable atmosphere. Our resistance to stressful situations is eventually eroded, leaving us prone to seemingly inexplicable accidents and misfortunes.

Often, the first area of our life in which we experience challenges is in our relationships with people with whom we are emotionally close or with whom we interact most of the time. We start complaining to our husbands or wives; our children seem out of control; our business partners suddenly appear incompetent. Everything gets on our nerves; we feel incapable of going on and ready to give up. Frustration becomes chronic.

Then the immune system, which is vital to protecting and maintaining our well-being, begins to weaken, and health problems gradually arise. This frustration and the slow decline of our well being affects our work, as well. Unable to maintain our concentration, we begin to forget things. Tired and frustrated, how motivated are we to invest energy in a new project or to undertake new risks? How effective is our decision-making ability when we are no longer clear and sharp?

The following case study illustrates the deleterious effects of negative environmental Qi on our health and business.

Case Study: Joan and Bill

Joan and Bill moved into their house in 1986. It was originally built in 1981, and by the time they moved in, the house had already seen three previous owners and a long period of vacancy.

The first couple moved in and divorced in less than a year; the second couple experienced severe health problems after moving in and moved out shortly thereafter; and the third couple moved there from another state upon the husband's acceptance of a fabulous new job in town; he was fired after a few months. They put the house back on the market and moved back to where they had come from.

After Joan and Bill moved in, they began to experience considerable difficulties: Joan began to show symptoms of depression, suffered severe energy loss, and underwent hand surgery twice to ameliorate a serious condition of the joints. Bill's business suffered serious financial problems, culminating with the loss of his job. He also underwent back surgery. Their daughter, Sandra, brought me in to review the home and also told me how difficult it now was for her to get along with both her mother and her boss at work. As soon as Sandra moved out of her parents' home, her life immediately took a turn for the better: She began dating a new man, and she accepted a new job with a higher salary in a significantly better work environment.

On visiting the house, I noticed a few interior design features that needed correction: A gigantic mirror on the headboard in the master bedroom, as well as a structural post right in front of the entry door. The headboard mirror reflected light from a window onto the couple's sleeping bodies, disturbing their rest and creating chaotic Qi, while the obtrusive post split the flow of Qi as it entered the room. This situation was resolved by removing the mirror and introducing a decorative screen between the post and the adjacent wall making the space similar to a solid wall around which Qi could move smoothly rather than splitting in two. This screen also helped create a division between the sleeping area and the retreat area.

The situation, however, was exacerbated by more fundamental complications. The house was built on a very steep hillside, provoking a sense of anxiety and anguish in the inhabitants, while depleting the entire building of good Qi, which leaked down the hillside slope. This fundamental problem was impossible to overcome, so after considering how adversely affected Joan and Bill already were, I suggested they move away as soon as the opportunity presented itself. In the interim, the changes helped Joan and Bill to feel much better. In particular, Joan experienced much more restful sleep, which in turn strengthened her immune system. Bill began a new business venture.

When we notice these kinds of negative changes in our health and in our feelings towards loved ones, we should consider the possibility that our living environment does not provide us with a good supply of Qi, or that our environment is "leaking" Qi somewhere. Let's now take a look at design features that one would be well advised to put in place or correct in order to establish a harmonious flow of Qi.

Shapes, Structures, Interiors, and Design

The Shape of the Building

When buying, building, or designing a space, we can understand a good deal about the Feng Shui of the building simply by observing its floor plan. In selecting the appropriate shape for our building, we can make a significant difference in the positive outcome of the entire project. Previously we looked at outside environmental factors, now we will focus on design features, which are similar to the attributes described in choosing lot shape. The following conditions are suggested for selecting the shape of the building.

Regularly Shaped Buildings

The most desirable shape of a building is a square or slightly rectangular overall perimeter. This balanced shape allows a favorable flow of Qi within the interior of the building. This feature gives the building an overall sense of balance.

Trapezoidal Building Shape

Buildings with a trapezoidal shape require different considerations. If the building has a wide facing side but a narrow sitting side, there will be no space to store Qi, which will therefore naturally flow out. It will thus be difficult for the inhabitants to retain wealth; they will be more prone to experiencing troubled emotions. Furthermore, since some of the rooms in the interior will be on an angle, instability in the room Qi will be created.

In a trapezoid-shaped building, if the sitting side is large and the facing side narrow, the building will be more effective in retaining the Qi, and therefore wealth, as long as the building satisfies other design criteria (described in the following sections).

Irregularly Shaped Buildings

Irregularly shaped buildings and floor plans are considered undesirable because they may create confusion in the inhabitants and Qi obstruction, stagnation, and instability. The same can be said for irregular harsh sections, particularly triangular. If we are evaluating an addition, these negative conditions can affect the entire building. However, minor room extensions or alterations that do not cause the overall perimeter to change are acceptable.

A triangular-shaped floor plan is considered highly undesirable because it doesn't have a stable sitting wall to rest upon. The inhabitants may experience constant conflicts and problems and a severely weakened ability to cope with stress.

Round and oval-shaped buildings promote a circular and fast Qi movement. This causes instability and continuous turnover in occupancy.

Houses with floor plan layouts resembling a Z, V, W, Y, X, C, or T should be avoided, since the Qi will have difficulty adapting to such irregular structures and sharp changes of direction.

About Regularly Shaped Buildings

Although, I mentioned earlier that square or rectangular shapes are preferable, this doesn't mean that all buildings should look like boring boxes with no character. What this concept means is that the primary perimeter or "envelope" of the building should resemble the balanced shape of a square or rectangle, rather than some erratic, irregular shape inside of which the Qi can not flow well. This is more likely to happen when we have very elongated and irregular shapes, perhaps constituting several different additions without overall planning.

Once we ensure that the overall inner or outer envelope has a regular shape, we can work on some minor stretching or indentations

The shape of a building determines the flow of Qi in its interior. Round shapes, or similar configurations (an octagon in this case) create instability; they lack solid backing for the Qi to rest on. This building hangs on a single, large post, which may cause further instability in the Qi of the building.

on the outside perimeter to both create movement in the façade and elevation and to make the floor plan design more interesting.

At an advanced level, these extensions and indentations can be done purposely to enlarge sections where the building's energy or the inner energy is more favorable than in other sections, or to accommodate particular design features related either to the building's or to the occupant's energy. However, this should be done cautiously and exclusively under the supervision of an expert.

The following floor plan shows an example where the architect,

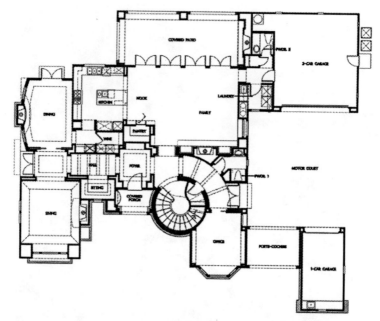

This custom home is designed according to Feng Shui principles and many factors were taken into account while designing it: Site features and layout, owner's date of birth, future date of construction, building orientation and the owner's requests in terms of functionality.

strictly following my Feng Shui guidelines, was able to both create an excellent floor plan with a unique style, while maintaining all the functions intact. As you can see, it is easy to see the traces of the regular rectangular shape underneath, while the design of the room flows harmoniously without becoming boring. (The garage section is an appendix to the main house.)

Quality of Soil for Feng Shui Purposes

When planning a new construction, for a proper structure and foundation, it is necessary to first appraise the soil. As mentioned earlier, it is preferable to start construction on well-leveled ground.

Poor sites include those in which the moisture content of the soil is not stable or where the soil may have been weakened because of seismic

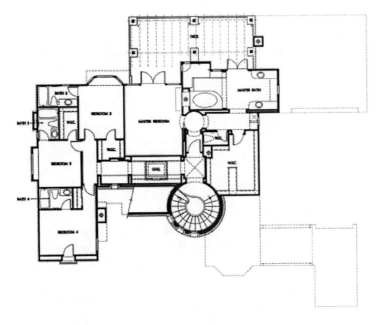

Although the overall envelope of the building is mildly rectangular, small extensions and indentations can create a more stylistically compelling final effect. (Dawson Hannouche Partners, Architecture Planning, Newport Beach, CA together with Feng Shui Architecture, Inc.; Beverly Hills, CA).

movement. This inconsistency can cause ground movement, distortion, and even collapse; which will affect the structure of the building and its Qi. An example would be land that is adjacent to a cliff where erosion can cause irregular soil movement to destabilize the foundation and eventually cause a collapse. One such area of Southern California is in the well-known Pacific Palisades, overlooking the ocean and the Pacific Coast Highway where rock slides are frequent.

It is not suitable to locate a building where there is soil that has been, naturally or by human interaction, impoverished of its natural life force. Among these are former locations of a burial site, a slaughter house, a power plant, or any other circumstance associated with death, violence, or any form of decay.

147

Structure

The structural design of a building should take into consideration soil conditions, weatherproofing, fire resistance, and thermal insulation, as well as soundproofing

The interior structure should be solid and stable, but not heavy and oppressive. Internal structural posts and beams should be incorporated inside the walls and ceilings/roof. Exposed, free-standing structural posts or beams break the Qi flow in a room and are therefore highly undesirable.

Solid foundations are very important to ensure the stability of a building and they should be planned accordingly. In the case of an older building, where conventional foundations are minimal or even nonexistent, an effort should be made to strengthen them and make them more stable. Otherwise, as in the case of a very old and poorly constructed building, it maybe often be preferable to level it and rebuild.

The Qi of houses built on stilts, however safe, is unstable because the wind will take advantage of the space that exists between the house and the ground; it will blow away the Qi. The same applies if only a portion of the house is built on stilts. That portion of the house will experience greater instability than the rest, and more so if the lower level is used as carport or garage.

Floor Plans and Interior Layout

Whether we are analyzing an existing building or are planning to design a new one, the interior layout is the next step in designing according to Feng Shui principles. By reducing the Qi obstruction, Qi depletion, and wind drafts in our design, we enhance the quality of our environment and our well being in it. The following are a number of conditions to avoid and suggestions to counteract any imbalances that can be used throughout the design of the building. If you adhere to the principles of Feng Shui during the design stage, there should be no need to correct anything later on.

Room Design

Regularly shaped rooms, square or rectangular, are generally preferable because they are easy to decorate, and we feel immediately at ease in them. Tilted or crooked walls intersecting at odd angles produce feelings of uneasiness in occupants as their personal Qi continuously tries to adjust to the uneven shape of the room. Symmetry in design is positive, but a balanced variety of shapes, forms and colors are even more preferable because it stimulates our sight while keeping us in a balanced state of mind. All in all, a functional interior layout favors beneficial air circulation as well as Qi flow.

The size of the rooms and ceiling heights should be well-proportioned. Narrow rooms with high ceilings may create a sense of pressure around the body, while a high ceiling will create an upward movement of Qi that may not be comfortable for people. Similarly, very large rooms with low ceilings can create a sense of pressure and oppression that will make occupants very uncomfortable and can cause them to feel stifled and pessimistic.

Doors and Windows

When designing rooms, we should be very mindful regarding positioning of the windows and doors, since they are openings through which the Qi enters and exits. The best plan is to design rooms that can retain as much life-force energy as possible allowing the occupants to access their full potential and avoid simultaneously creating any stagnation that could spoil the Qi.

Doors should not be aligned directly opposite windows or other doors, as drafts literally blow the Qi out of the house before it has time to spread its beneficial energy through the building. If doors and windows are aligned, drafts can be avoided simply by opening only one of them at a time, using curtains or opaque materials, or placing a wall partition or a screen that is compatible with the room's size and design in between them.

A good plan would be to try to create a sheltering area diagonally

When a garage or a carport is located on the lower floor of a building, underneath a bedroom or in the main part of the house, the vibration created by cars entering and exiting will generate an instability in the Qi in that part of the house. It is preferable to locate a garage or carport on the side.

opposite the entry door where the Qi can gather and to plan the windows so that they are not aligned with the door and therefore do not interrupt the flow in the solid gathering space. This sheltering area can effectively accommodate a bed, a desk, or furnishings for any other activity that may require the support of life-force energy.

Glass Walls and Skylights

Low windows do not retain the Qi well in a room. Glass walls are even less favorable in this respect because they may not sufficiently support the Qi in the room.

Skylight windows can be used to increase natural sunlight in areas that would otherwise be very dark. Ideal locations for skylights can be bathrooms, kitchens, garages, and, on a case-by-case basis, stairways. It is better not to use skylights in bedrooms or other rooms where we spend extensive amounts of time. In fact, a glass opening

An arrangement where doors are aligned with each other or with a window, causes Qi to move in a direct line from opening to opening, preventing it from spreading equally throughout the entire floor (Leesburg, VA).

in the ceiling tends to attract the Qi in the room, creating an upward movement in the flow pattern that can be uncomfortable for the human physiology. Especially large skylights above beds can result in great discomfort.

Square Footage

The square footage of a building should be proportionate to the activity and number of people in the house. Houses with large

151

When windows are very large and close to the floor, they will not retain the room's Qi efficiently therefore causing dispersion and depletion. It is preferable to place windows high enough above the floor level to properly contain the beneficial Qi (Leesburg, VA)

dimensions and few occupants may tend to feel cold and lonely. This is because some of the rooms may remain unused for a prolonged amount of time, and therefore start to build up Yin, stagnant Qi, a condition that is never desirable as we have seen earlier.

The use of warm colors, pleasant lighting, tranquil sounds (such as water flow, music, or gentle grandfather-clock chimes), and plants can serve to keep the Qi moving and avoid stagnation due to inactivity. Furniture also helps in reducing this feeling of loneliness, but beware of using antiques, since they also posses Yin Qi and may therefore end up making things worse.

On the other hand, small houses with many occupants may feel overwhelming and chaotic due to a lack of privacy. In this case the amount and size of the furniture should be smaller in order to provide more free space for the Qi to flow.

If the upper floor has larger dimensions then the lower, this will cause pressure and could overpower the Qi in the lower levels. In this case, the larger upper floor is overpowering the Qi at the main entrance and garage entrance, preventing it from bringing its beneficial effects inside the building.

Upper Floors

The lower and upper floors should be clearly defined in their functions, separate but easily accessible. Poor definition of lower and upper floors to the point of confusion is a sure sign that the building's Qi isn't flowing properly, and some, or most, rooms are likely not receiving an adequate supply of Qi.

If the dimensions of the upper floor are considerably smaller than the lower, the upper area will have a sense of instability and it will lack of protection from the surrounding wind—more so if the walls are mostly inset with glass.

When the dimensions of the upper floor are greater then the lower, the upper floor will create a sense of overbearing pressure on the entering Qi, particularly over the doors and windows.

Additions

Room additions should be connected and accessible to the main house, with the exception of guest houses and pool houses, to create a smooth path through all parts of the building so as to promote a more favorable flow of Qi. They should also be integrated as much as possible to the pre-existing building in terms of floor level and roof level, color, material, window and door frames, etc.

Connecting Rooms

Long, narrow, and dark hallways are not favorable because they dissipate and oppress the Qi, creating confusion in the occupants.

They should always be well lit and well proportioned in width and ceiling height.

They are better when wide and spacious and as short as possible. Maze-like hallways create a sense of oppression in the Qi flow of the building and consequently in its occupants.

The entry door to a room should not be placed at the end of a long corridor, since the Qi funneled from the corridor and entering the room is too strong and may become harmful to the occupants. This is particularly important for a bedroom.

Design Features

As mentioned earlier, "designer" houses may or may not have good Feng Shui. It is preferable to prioritize comfort above originality and harmony above artistry. However, a comfortable and harmonious original design can still incorporate all or most of the more important Feng Shui characteristics while maintaining an artistic look.

Stairs

Staircases should be pleasant to the eyes in their design and also easy to climb. When overly narrow, curvy, steep, or dark, they become

"Designer" houses may have irregular shapes and other features that are contrary to Feng Shui principles. These can be balanced by selecting a proper orientation and siting before construction.

uncomfortable and they can create constraint in the Qi movement that will affect the distribution of the Qi between the floors.

Well-lit staircases with wide, shallow steps and broad landings at both ends, which are not aligned with any doors leading to rooms, allow benevolent Qi to flow between floors. Having doors at both ends of a stairway is not considered a favorable condition. The momentum of the intense climbing or descending Qi will force it against the doors and into the rooms, and this is not the preferred way for Qi to enter a room because it is too strong and too aggressive.

Additionally, if a staircase is aligned with the entry door or with a window, the Qi will leak out of the house, causing a loss of opportunity and money.

Roofs and Ceilings

Complicated roofing can be oppressive for a building and heavy components can reflect a sense of pressure and domination that may result in a difficulty to achieve one's personal and financial goals.

155

Favorable staircases are wide and well-lit, with shallow steps and broad landings at both ends.

Decorative roof features can be used with common sense to enrich a building's design without interfering with its potential for the well being of the inhabitants.

Sudden changes in ceiling height or floor level when moving from room to room through a sequence of steps interrupt the flow of Qi in the house and could waste our energy as we struggle to adjust to the erratic Qi flow. Such irregular ceiling and floor designs are better avoided and our energy better conserved for more constructive purposes.

Beams and Posts

Ceiling beams that lie directly over an entrance or bed, often considered a prestigious design component, can cause "Qi wave pressure," a direct and intense downward flow, by channeling heavy Qi against a person entering the room or lying in bed. Instilling feelings of oppression and uneasiness, heavy ceiling beams can place unfavorable pressure on the inhabitants' health and relationships; it can have adverse consequences. If beams are already in place and cannot be removed, the easiest and most effective solution is to flatten the ceiling surface by using drywall to construct a lower ceiling under the beams.

Free-standing columns should be avoided since they break the flow of Qi in the room. If they are necessary for the structural support, they should be round to avoid affecting the interior with sharp corners. It is, however, preferable to incorporate them as part of the walls in the building floor plan prior to construction.

Posts that are partially imbedded in a wall and protrude from it, whether in a corner or in the middle of the wall, create "pointing Sha" in the direction of the outer corners. It is not recommended to locate a desk or a bed in line with these pointing corners. Similar to a ceiling beam, a post that creates irregularities in a wall's flat surface produces horizontal wave pressure, compressing the Qi and cutting it into two parts, thus disturbing the room's natural energy flow.

Internal Sha

Pointed corners and sharp angles directed toward important areas of the house, such as the main entrance or the bed, are inauspicious sources of Sha and they should be avoided as much as possible or at least screened with a plant or a small fountain.

Mirrors and Other Décor Elements

Mirrors can be very effective devices to enlarge our perceptions of spaces and to relieve pressure from feelings of claustrophobia. A small living room can be brought to life with a mirror reflecting a beautiful view. However, it is advisable not to place a mirror where it will continuously reflect the people who spend a great deal of time there, as in a bedroom. Facing a reflection all day can be distracting and extremely frustrating because of the continuous bombardment of electromagnetic waves amplified by the mirror.

Fireplaces should have screens and vent covers to eliminate wind draft in the room when they are not being used.

Design patterns used for walls, floors, and furniture should be harmonious and coordinated. Excessively convoluted patterns, mismatched colors, and harsh-looking design features take away from the feeling of balance and harmony in a room.

The cleanliness and tidiness of the interior is a very important factor. This is even more important in the presence of pets. Life-force energy tends to loose its strength and become heavy and stagnant when rooms are dusty, stuffy, or smelly.

Chapter 9

INTERIOR DECORATION

Interior decoration is the art of enriching the architectural shell with colors, materials and lights to create a comfortable sense of harmony. Although interior design can be very effective in creating pleasant interiors, some Feng Shui tips can be crucial to further enhance the design by enhancing the building's natural 'energy'.

Light and Shade

Light and shade are the most identifiable features of the environment that can be read in terms of Yin and Yang and, as with every other polarity-related feature, they should always be balanced relative to the personalities, ages, and activities of the people living in those environments.

Each stage of life may have a different predisposition toward a more Yang or a more Yin environment. For example, children are often drawn to bright colors, lights and strong emotions. This is an expression of their predominantly Yang qualities. An elderly person instead may be drawn more to subtle colors and a more shady environment and may have more inward, Yin tendencies.

For children, a Yang environment is generally preferable. To create a Yin environment for a child may not be a great idea, as it may damage the child's personal energy balance. Similarly, to create a very Yang environment for elderly people may not be a good idea either as it may result in over-stimulation, which could put a strain on their energy levels.

The overall character of a person also dictates Yin and Yang; some may be more attracted to Yang and others to Yin. For example, although children may have a more Yang energy in general, some may be more Yang and others a bit more Yin in character. Some characters may also have an overall higher predisposition for Yang or for Yin at various stages of their lives, so part of customizing an interior is also being able to relate to individual requests and needs.

Yin Interiors

The most tangible Yin environment is a dark room or a house where there is insufficient light to allow the inhabitants to feel vibrant and cheerful. This excess of Yin energy causes the Qi to feel tired and heavy and to stagnate throughout the house, as well as in the human body.

Light from every available source must be added to re-establish the balance between light and shade.

Crowded, dark, and stuffy rooms produce feelings of confusion and frustration. It is commonly known that in order to avoid illness and depression we need to be exposed to both natural sunlight and fresh air.

An area where sunlight may enter rooms directly for at least a few hours each day is always preferable. It affects the room's occupants positively because it energizes or rejuvenates the Qi in the room. Although light bulbs can be efficient substitutes for natural sunlight, it is best to have light from natural sources whenever possible.

Light colors and glossy finishes, as well as reflective glass surfaces, can also be introduced to increase Yang energy.

If the room is not a bedroom, a proportionate number of decorative mirrors may be introduced, as well. A well-placed mirror may increase the light in a dark room and alleviate feelings of pressure, especially if it reflects a pleasant view. Reflective panels in gold or silver leaf can act as mirror substitutes and create a more elegant look.

During the summer or in a hot climate, a small fountain with

A skylight can be very helpful in allowing natural sunlight into rooms otherwise too dark (courtesy of Move Italia).

moving water may also be introduced to eliminate the Qi stagnation, but this is a secondary measure to be taken after the light aspects have been balanced.

In critical situations, constructing a window or a skylight may also be helpful. However, it is preferable not to install a skylight in a bedroom above the bed area, because the upward movement of Qi may create unstable sleep patterns.

Also, before installing any window or skylight, it is preferable to consult with a Feng Shui expert, because of the possible side effects related to the Invisible Qi. Depending on the overall quality of the Invisible Qi in the room, that room can be altered positively or negatively by opening a wall or ceiling to install a window or a skylight.

Yang Interiors

At the other end of the spectrum, an environment presenting too many Yang characteristics may also pose problems if it is strongly unbalanced. Yang interiors generally have an excessive number of windows and/or glass doors, or even glass walls, allowing the sun's powerful radiation to be present every moment of the day. Inhabitants constantly exposed to excessive light often become too stimulated by the rapid and intense Qi movement and tend to be edgy and overly reactive.

If an excess of sunlight pervades the bedroom, the inhabitants may suffer from severe insomnia or from a chronic lack of restful sleep.

Too much light is often the case in many houses with beautiful natural views, where eagerness about maintaining the view causes the designers to forget to balance the interiors. This error creates the so-called "fishbowl" effect. This consideration is also particularly critical in the lower floors of urban residential buildings, where passers-by outside at street level can look in.

A glass-walled office environment where employees have no privacy during their work hours and thus constantly feel pushed and stimulated by their coworkers' intrusive attention can be another example of an excessively Yang environment. The same can be said for a unit in an apartment block.

To correct such situations, it is critical to introduce curtains or a screening system that allows occupants to be open to or shielded from the exterior environment. When planning a new design, it is imperative to consider a proper balance of solid and see-through walls.

More subdued colors and matte surfaces are elements that can be used to absorb some of the excess light in order to re-establish balance in the interior decoration.

Colors and Materials: Selecting the Color Palette

At a professional level, the use of color and materials takes into account the building's orientation, time of construction, and the proposed occupants.

The overall color scheme of a house should be chosen based on the building's orientation. Depending on its sitting and facing positions, the house will belong to one of the Five Elements. I

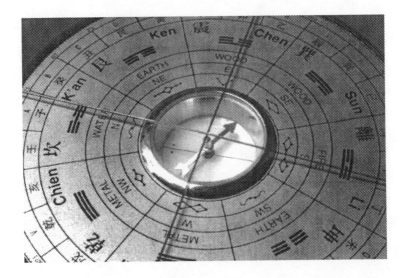

To select an appropriate color palette for a house, it is advisable to use a compass to determine the building's orientation. The color palette is related to the inherent energy of the building, which in turn is related to the direction in which the house sits and faces (see chart).

recommend using a compass to evaluate the exact orientation of your house. A Lo Pan compass is ideal, but if one is not available, a good hiking compass can also be used. Traditionally, the sitting position, always located opposite the facing position, is the one that determines the building's trigram and element.

The facing position is the direction the front of the building faces independent of the location of the entry door. The entry door, in fact, could be located in the front, on the side, or in the back of the building.

Each of the eight directions consists of 45 degrees and should be fairly easy to identify with the compass, starting with 0 degrees (North), in the center of the 45-degree pie shape associated with the North direction. The North section, in brief, extends from 337.5 degrees to 22.5 degrees.

According to the Five Elements Theory, the element to which the house belongs determines the most appropriate colors and materials that should be used to support the overall energy of the building. Productive elements should be used, while those that are reductive or domineering should be avoided.

To assist us in choosing the preferable colors and materials for a house, we can use the table below. Also, in order to help identify the building's element, I have listed the sitting and facing directions:

Facing	Sitting	Degree	Element	Color	Material
North	South	157.5-202.5	Fire	All shades of red All shades of green	Wood
Northeast	Southwest	202.5-247.5	Earth	All earth tones All shades of red	Natural stone Brick
East	West	247.5-292.5	Metal	All shades of white All shades of gray All earth tones	Copper, Brass Steel Stone, Brick
Southeast	Northwest	292.5-337.5	Metal	All shades of white All shades of gray All earth tones	Copper, Brass Steel Stone, Brick
South	North	337.5-22.5	Water	All shades of blue All shades of white All shades of gray	Copper, Brass Steel
Southwest	Northeast	22.5-67.5	Earth	All earth tones All shades of red	Natural stone Brick
West	East	67.5-112.5	Wood	All shades of green All shades of blue	Wood
Northeast	Southwest	112.5-157.5	Wood	All shades of green All shades of blue	Wood

Table 4. Ideal colors and materials related to a house's orientation

The Fire Element House

A house that belongs to the Fire element can be painted using all shades of red, burgundy, hot pink, or bright orange. Lighter shades of the same pigments are also acceptable. All shades of green can also be favorable, since green is related to Wood, which is productive to Fire.

Fire-related accessories such as fire places or candles can be used in the interior, although the best position should be selected under an expert's supervision. Finally, the building will do well if built with wood or with wood finishing, but it is also important to remember balance at all times and to avoid excessively dark or overwhelming colors.

Earth materials, such as stone or brick, and earth colors are also acceptable since Fire and Earth are productive in the Five Elements Theory; however, do not overuse them since Earth takes away from Fire's strength. Metal elements and colors are also not appropriate for this type of house, since the two elements clash with each other.

Water colors and materials are definitely not recommended because the Water element dominates and extinguishes the Fire's energy, thereby reducing the house's energy and its positive effects on the occupants.

The Earth Element House

A house that belongs to the Earth element is versatile because it can use a large selection of earth tones, including yellow, beige, tan, brown, and orange. Shades of red can also be used both in the exterior and interior (Fire is productive to Earth). We can pick soft earth tones like beige and tan for the exterior, for example, and then go wild with yellows and oranges in the interior. In this case it is important to base the shades on the principle colors and use same color pigments with varied levels of saturation to obtain different shades of the same colors. It is important to have a consistency of color both inside and outside. Pottery, stones of

In this designer house, the structure and interior/exterior treatment consists primarily of the Earth element, in shape of concrete blocks. Although the Earth element is favorable for this building, in this case we are witnessing an excess of the Earth element which may cause a stagnation of the Yin Qi.

every kind, ceramic tiles, and clay sculptures are effective as earthy materials and for exteriors, natural stone and brick are the best choices.

According to the Five Elements Theory, Metal materials and colors can be used, although we may use them carefully, since Metal drains the strength of the Earth element. Also, Water accessories and colors are not as favorable, and the Wood element's green palette is definitely to be avoided since it will dominate the building's energy and its occupants.

The Metal Element House

A house belonging to the Metal element can use a variety of cool tones, preferably whites and grays. Beautiful natural metal elements such as copper, brass, and stainless steel can also be used for artistic and tasteful finishing and detailing. In addition, according to the Five Elements Theory, Earth produces Metal, therefore earth tones and stone or brick elements can also be combined to strengthen the building's natural energy.

Mirrors as well as the majority of large reflective materials, which are currently used in the construction industry, shouldn't be overused, since they are not considered metal elements.

Unless recommended by an expert on a case-by-case analysis, it is preferable not to overdue the use of any Water-related accessory or color in this house, since Water will reduce the building's natural energy.

Shades of green are not favorable either, and shades of red and Fire elements should be avoided, since they dominate the Metal energy.

The Water Element House

For the Water-element house, we can use any shade of blue (or blue-based purple such as lavender), as well as whites and grays. In theory, black can also be used; however, it is not generally recommended because it may take away from the building's natural radiance since it is so dark. The Water element can be used in both the interior and exterior, and as far as construction materials go, metal materials such as copper, stainless steel, and brass can be used for elegant finishing and detailing.

For this kind of house, shades of red will not appear particularly appealing, since the Fire tones are dominated by the building's natural energy.

Wood and greenery are more acceptable in and around this house because Water and Wood enhance each other's Qi in the Five Elements Theory. Earth tones, colors, and materials are not recommended either since the Earth element will dominate the building's natural energy.

The Wood Element House

To decorate the Wood element house, we can use any shade of green or blue. As in the Water house, black can also be used; however, the same cautionary note applies to this very dark color.

With respect to construction material, woods of all kinds, especially dark woods, can be used for elegant finishing and detailing. Real plants, trees, and flower beds are fine in the interior and exterior. The energy of this building is also positively enhanced by the use of water features, as long as carefully positioned by an expert.

The Wood element house works well with shades of red, since Wood and Fire are linked together in the productive cycle, however, since Fire tends to reduce the building's natural energy it is preferable to not overuse them. Also, metals or white and gray shades shouldn't be used since they aggressively dominate the building's overall energy and its occupants.

More About Colors, Materials and Decor

What I have been describing so far is the overall color palette for the building according to its element. At an advanced level, the expert knows that there may be other factors influencing the color or the materials that can be used in a room. These may vary from room to room and also differ from building to building. This is a consequence of the building's individual energy, based on the time of construction, and on the energy of the occupants based on their year of birth. An experienced professional should be able to tell when and how these other factors combine with the information presented above.

When a building is decorated with its most harmonious colors and materials, its energy tends to attract people who are compatible with it on an energy level, which is often manifested as an immediate sense of comfort.

On the other hand, when a building belongs to a specific element, but is decorated with materials and color schemes that belong to another element, it tends to attract people who resonate with the second element because the overall most immediately recognizable "energy radiance" is given off by the decor. In spite of this immediate feeling of attraction, the basic energy of the building will not be in harmony with its occupants and will therefore not support them as efficiently in the long run.

The "Three Powers Rule" Applied to Interior Decoration

In the beginning of this book, in order to define the three main levels of the life-force energy, we described the Three Powers: Heaven Qi, Human Qi, and Earth Qi.

The three levels of the life-force energy "rule" are also applied to interior decoration. The ceilings represent the Heaven Qi, the floor the Earth Qi and the walls, along with anything else between ceiling and floor, pertains to the realm of Human Qi.

I would also like to point out a connection between the Yin and Yang polarities, the ceiling being the highest point of the Yang section in the Tai Qi symbol and the floor the lowest point of the Yin section.

In selecting the color scheme for our rooms, these concepts should be remembered and applied in the following manner:

• The floor should be always darker than the ceiling and the walls.
• The ceiling should always be the lightest color of the three
• The walls should be somewhere in between, not darker than the floor and not lighter than the ceiling.

This will create a sense of harmony and consistency in the overall Qi flow of the room.

I often encounter houses that have very light hardwood floors (oak or pine) or carpeting, with dark walls. Although the effect can be quiet pleasant and original at first, in the long run the darkness of the walls tends to create a feeling of heaviness. It is important to remember the Three Powers rule and to use either a darker shade of flooring, being mindful of not creating a dark room, or a lighter shade on the walls. In particular, ceilings that are darker than the floors should be avoided.

The idea behind this concept comes, once again, from the Yin/Yang theory: the Yang energy rises to the top of the symbol with the culmination of Yang at its fullest at the top, while Yin decreases, with the culmination of Yin at its fullest at the bottom. Consequently, the upper part of a room, especially the ceiling, should be lighter in color, while the lower part, the floor, should be darker.

Yin and Yang Polarities

Years ago I was invited to visit a showroom for the display of new contemporary-style furniture.

The design of the showroom was beautiful, but in order to create a dramatic and theatrical effect, the designer had chosen to paint the ceiling black and the floor pure white throughout the entire display area.

Needless to say, this effect was very dramatic. However, a few minutes after entering the showroom, I noticed a chill on both my shoulders and back. This effect didn't diminish, but increased during the thirty minutes or so that it took for me to walk around the floor and admire the new products. By the end of my visit, I was very uncomfortable and I began feeling unusually disoriented.

About ten minutes after I left the place, I started feeling better. I then became aware that, while I was in that space, my body had matched the ambient flow of Qi. Because of the reversed Yin and Yang polarities expressed by the color placement, the Yang polarity was flowing principally from the ceiling to the floor in a reverse pattern, rather than flowing from the floor to the ceiling as it should have. I realized that my body, affected by the energy flow of the room, had begun reversing its own Qi-flow pattern which was why I felt so uncomfortable.

This is typically what happens when we have ceilings that are darker than floors. The darker the ceiling, the more oppressed the Qi will become causing it to flow toward the bottom of the room, creating a feeling of heaviness and discomfort in the people living there.

Remembering Yin and Yang

It is important to use common sense and practice moderation in the color and materials for a building. Remember that, with the

Yin and Yang energy polarity, balance is always the key. Too often we are fooled by appearances and think that a lot of a good thing is even better than a little. We can have a tasteful use of appropriate colors and materials and can also incorporate small quantities of other elements to create an overall harmony. The essence of a Yin and Yang awareness is balance, so we should take care not to overdo anything.

Case Study: A Beach House in Malibu

A few years ago, when I visited a beach house in Malibu designed in 1929 by a famous local architect, I was utterly captivated by the astonishing ocean view and the very charming Spanish architecture of the building. Most of all, I was overwhelmed by the enduring quality of the colors and materials used in the home, still perfectly preserved after 70 years. The owners of this beach house also owned an adjacent tile factory, and the house used to be a tile showcase: Every floor and many of the walls were decorated with tiles of various shapes, sizes, colors, and patterns. The dominant color, however, was a natural burnt-red clay, with perfectly coordinated paintings, furniture, and decorative objects.

On account of its lovely design and its perfect condition, this estate is today a national treasure; but from a Feng Shui point of view, the house suffers from a tremendous domination of the Earth element. The house sits Southwest, therefore belonging to the Kun trigram and, as I have described previously, it naturally belongs to the Earth element in its overall energy nature.

Since Kun, having three broken lines, is the most Yin of all the trigrams, it is evident that in the building's inherent nature is a dominant Yin energy, which is increased by the presence of extensive Earth elements, embodied in clay, pottery, and tiles, which are definitely the most appropriate materials for this kind of house.

Indeed, upon entering, I felt as though I had stepped into the cool shade of a cave. Considering the home's exposure to California's hot summers, the extreme Yin quality of the home made a sort of interior balance to the Yang quality of the sunny exterior. However, during winter, it is possible that its residents may have suffered from a chilly and uncomfortable coolness, typical of excessive Yin features.

As Kun, by virtue of its Yin quality which is also associated with the feminine energy—the matriarch or the mother—the house was therefore very supportive of the female gender. In excess, however, Kun may produce loneliness and feelings of emptiness and particularly does not attract men, which resonate with a more Yang energy's environment. Coincidentally, due to premature deaths of male family members, women had mainly occupied the house.

What would we do if we encountered a house like this? According to the general energy floor plan of the building, we could introduce Yang elements to counterbalance its extreme Yin nature. For example, we might introduce the Wood element: hardwood floors are definitely warmer and more embracing than tile floors, and many areas, such as bedrooms, living rooms, dining rooms or family rooms, would benefit from their warmth. In general, tile floors are more appropriate for a kitchen, bathroom, and utility room. As Spanish tile is very water resistant, it can also be used for patios, gardens, and swimming pool areas.

Lighter tones, such as off white or ivory, may be used in the decoration to reflect more light. Windows and skylights may also be introduced to bring in natural sunlight. Even the color of upholstery and carpeting or rugs can play an important role in warming up a room. According to the building's energy, red or burgundy decorations may also inject a strong touch of warm color and at the same time strengthen the energy of the building without overdoing the Earth-element decor.

Balance Is the Key

Another extremely Yin situation is in the High Tech style, where we encounter an environment rich in metal, black and gray hues, and other cool tones. Our energy tends to be drained away in such a Yin environment, simply because there is almost a total absence of the life-supporting Yang energy. In fact, the primary

Yin/Yang polarity factor to bear in mind here is that life requires Yang energy, while death feeds on Yin energy. Thus, when designing houses for the living, we must provide Yang energy, while when designing for the deceased we must make Yin energy available.

Balance, however, is always the key. As already stated, excessively Yang houses can also pose problems. For example, we may encounter houses that are too "bright," both in their appearance and in their affect which is not a desirable situation since they will require a bit of Yin to achieve balance and harmony. This also follows from the Third Principle of Yin and Yang given by the Yellow Emperor, which we discussed earlier: Yin and Yang are opposites, and each fulfills and complements the other.

Case Study: Cynthia's Apartment

Cynthia's apartment had off-white walls and carpets and large, nearly wall-size windows. It contained almost no furniture except for a dark green sofa in the living room, a glass table with four metal chairs in the dining room, and a low Japanese-style futon bed in the bedroom. She expressed to me how uncomfortable she felt: *"I feel like this isn't my place; I cannot focus, I do not have a romantic life, and I'm feeling very unhappy."*

Although I was struck by the stark interiors when I walked in, a deeper analysis revealed no problems with the outside environment or with the building's energy field. So I advised her to add some decorations and furniture to the space. I suggested she hang some of her favorite pictures and prints, a few of which I noticed were lying on the floor. I also encouraged her to bring in curtains to screen the huge windows and introduce plants to soften the harsh, pointed corners.

I suggested she also decorate the house with pictures of family and friends and install vases with her favorite flowers. By infusing the space with her own taste and personal touches, she could make the house her own and not feel so alone and unhappy. We all need to create a comfortable environment where we recognize our own

173

presence and feel comfortable while working or entertaining. This makes the difference between a house and home.

Our Houses Must Feel Like Home

Too often we get hung up on creating a house that looks as we think it should: one that provides a showcase to impress our guests or acts as a strong statement of our design beliefs. This concept only works if these are real expressions of who we are, otherwise we may discover that a showcase design is alien to our intrinsic self, or our moods and tastes may change and, in such case, we should not hesitate to change the decor. Our goal should be to create an environment that expresses our true nature and makes us feel the most at home.

I am reminded of a friend who was heartbroken when his fiancée left him and moved out of their house. "She is taking all the furniture and the art objects. I am left facing bare walls," he wailed desperately. A few months later, however, he seemed happy and rejuvenated, and when I asked him how his house was coming along, he smiled and declared emphatically, "I am so happy! I got a new sofa and a new bedroom set. And I finally hung my favorite pictures and prints. They have been in the closet for years, just because my former fiancée never liked them. It felt good seeing them after such a long time. In all these years, this is truly the first time I really feel like this is MY home."

Sometimes, even distressing breakups can bring some advantages, especially if we reclaim our homes by decorating them with our own unique and special style.

I remember many years ago a teacher I had in architecture school said: "You can always tell people's capacity for love [of themselves and others]," she said, "by the way they love their homes."

Chapter	ROOM
10	BY
	ROOM

The creation of a good floor plan and a good design is crucial to a successful project. To accomplish that, this chapter will address favorable and unfavorable design features and conditions which should be taken into consideration for each room.

Throughout the building's design, you can express your unique lifestyle in the layout of the room. While a large formal living room and dining room may imply that that you like to entertain, a comfortable and spacious family room may mean that your family prefers to spend lot of time gathering together in a more private way. With a good Feng Shui design, these habits and functions come together in a floor plan that joins all the functions harmoniously and maintains a good flow of life-force energy, room by room, throughout the building.

On the other hand, certain rooms require more attention than others; various functions require more or less time spent in their corresponding rooms and therefore more or less interaction with that particular room's energy. Needless to say, particular attention should be paid to designing rooms used for larger blocks of time, such as bedrooms, or particular areas, such as entrances, that are crucial to the entire building's energy flow.

In order to design harmonious houses, the very first step is to create a harmonious floor plan. Although the design of elevations is generally of secondary importance, it should also be planned harmoniously.

Main Entry, Side Entry, Garage Entry

The main entry is the focal point for the entire house; it is the principal entrance through which the Qi flows and gathers inside the building. Unfavorable features may become obstacles to the entering Qi and deplete the house of its energy; they should be avoided as much as possible.

Choosing an appropriate design is crucial to ensuring that the entering Qi is positive and will enhance the prosperity and happiness of its inhabitants. Furthermore, because the entrance is where the Qi transitions from outside to inside, the considerations are not just limited to the physical door itself: they also include the surrounding external environment as well as the internal features.

Outside the Door

The area in front of the building should be open and unobstructed in order to allow a favorable Qi to gather and flow freely into the building. The pathway to the entrance should also be well defined.

There should not be any trees, telephone or power poles located in front of the entrance, and any other obstruction to the Qi flow should be avoided. Any obstacle that can create an obstruction or a depletion of the entering Qi will end up affecting the entire household.

Any unpleasant view from a home should also be avoided, since it would create a Visual Sha for the occupants. Police stations, cemeteries, hospitals, nightclubs, courthouses and other sources of disturbance to the family life should be avoided.

Any "poisoned arrow" or sharp corner pointing toward the front door should not be visible from the entrance. If such features exist, they should be screened with plants, or since these features are so unfavorable, it may be wiser to change the location of the entrance.

It is preferable to have an open space in front of the main entrance. In this case, a structural post is obstructing it, causing a break in the Qi flow.

Location

When working with a Feng Shui expert, he or she will recommend the best entrance location within the context of the building's energy profile. This choice is based on what I have just mentioned in addition to the inhabitants' birth years and the building's Invisible Qi.

As most experts who are knowledgeable about the Invisible Qi influences are aware, the location of the entrance has the power to increase or reduce positive energy effects on the entire household. If the entrance is located in a good area, the

A narrow and dark entrance and foyer, especially with hanging features, will cause the entering Qi to stagnate and become oppressed, bringing unfavorable effects to the occupants of the house.

occupants will experience prosperity and opportunity, but if it is located in an unfavorable area, the occupants may experience more difficulties in their lives.

The ideal location for the main entrance follows the natural flow of the building's energy. Entrances at the side of a house often create a sense of confusion in the flow of Qi in the interior.

Bathrooms, garages, or often messy kitchens, shouldn't be visible from the entrance, particularly from the main entrance.

Entrance Design

The entrance should be proportionate in size with the house, neither overly high nor overly low.

The main entrance should be prominent and should also be located in a favorable quadrant so that it can be used at all times to bring prosperity to the house.

The entrance should not be positioned under ceiling beams

When the main entrance consists of a glass door that is also directly aligned with a glass back door, the Qi entering the house will pass through and exit immediately.

or other heavy hanging objects in the interior or exterior. This tends to create a sense of pressure and oppression on the entering Qi that could affect the entire household.

Ideally, it is better to avoid any alignment between the front doors and the back doors, including sliding glass doors, large windows, and glass walls. Once the favorable Qi enters, it will tend to rush out the opposite opening without having time to flow throughout the building and distribute its benevolent effects.

It is also better for the entrance not to be in a round tower element, since this may have a negative effect on male residents of the house.

When a main entrance is located in a round foyer or in a tower-like feature, this is considered unfavorable since it may negatively affect a male homeowner.

Foyer

It is preferable to have a foyer area in proximity to the main entrance. This allows the Qi flowing in from the door to gather in the foyer area and to be distributed from there to the entire house through hallways and doors in a smooth configuration often referred to as *Ming Tong*.

The foyer area should be proportionate to the size of the house, particularly to the lower floor: if it is too big, the Qi will disperse too much; if it is too small, the entering Qi will not be sufficient to support the entire house.

Stairs

Avoid placing staircases too close to the entrance. The Qi will either rush out the door from the upper floor or leak precipitously into the basement. This effect is greater if the starting point of the stairway is facing the front door directly.

A slightly curving stairway can enhance the entrance area by defining the foyer and gathering Qi around the entrance before meandering through the rest of the house. In this case, be mindful not to place it too close to the door.

Secondary or Side Entrances

Secondary entrances are very popular nowadays to access the back garden or to carry the groceries from the driveway to the kitchen. According to Feng Shui when a house has several entrances, it can confuse the entering Qi, especially if both entrances are in the front of the house. Therefore, a secondary entrance should never be placed in the front of the building. Ideally, it should be in a less visible position and it should be used only for a limited function.

A skilled Feng Shui expert may actually recommend against the position of a secondary entrance, based on the occupants' birth years or on the building's Invisible Qi energy, if a potential for the secondary entrance to have a more positive effect than the main one is not foreseen. However, these decisions should only be made under expert supervision.

Garage Entries

The garage entry is also very popular nowadays, and although the garage may not be considered part of the house per se, cars entering and exiting can impact energy in that particular section of the house. The Qi entering from there will affect the building just as much as it will when it enters through the main entrance, or even more so if this garage entrance is used the most. It is preferable to have the access from the garage to the house open into the foyer area as well, possibly in a position where it is not immediately visible from the main entrance or with a door that blends in with the surrounding wall and is not very obvious.

In contemporary homes, entrances from a garage are often used as much if not more frequently than main entrances. When planning a new building, an alternate entrance's location and the effects it could have on the building and its occupants must be taken into account.

Case Study: A Malibu Estate

I consulted for a large (over 10,000 sq. ft.) house in Malibu, and despite the house's huge facade, the entry door was very small, about the size of a typical apartment door. The stagnation of Qi in the entry area was very evident. As the size of the entrance was much too small for the house, the amount of Qi entering was low and stagnant; it was unable to create and sustain prosperity and well being for the occupants.

Moreover, the round foyer was open to the formal dining and living room, and therefore, upon entering the front door, one could immediately see the view from the large windows in those areas. The new owners were planning some structural remodeling, so given the opportunity for substantial changes, I advised them to enlarge the entrance to make it more proportionate to the size of the house. I also recommended that they create some wall partitions between the entry door and the dining/living room areas in order to create more privacy and to allow the Qi to gather in the foyer area and then flow into the entire house through doors and hallways, rather than rush toward the big windows and disperse through those openings.

The beautiful final effect was created using sanded glass sliding doors, and their translucent surface allowed the light from the big living room window to brighten the foyer area while creating a physical obstacle to the depletion of the Qi, yet allowing it to flow freely through the entire house.

Dining Rooms, Living Rooms, and Family Rooms

When designing a good Feng Shui layout, living, dining, and family rooms have secondary priority to the entrances, bedrooms and home offices. However, for an active home life, it is advisable to follow some basic guidelines to ensure that these rooms are in harmony with the rest of the house.

Dining Rooms

The dining room is the typical place for meals and family gatherings; it is where most people interact socially. A clean and semi-formal design will help create a serene atmosphere.

Living Rooms

The living room should have a more formal appearance, be open to receive guests, and be well kept at all times. Though the living room is often the place where we relax and watch TV (especially if we do not have a family room), it is also the area where we interact most with our guests. Therefore, care must be taken to make this living space as open, inviting, and comfortable to visitors as possible. As it is also often the first room we enter in the house, and we are the first to benefit from the serene atmosphere and comfort of this space.

Family Rooms

The family room, on the other hand, is the area where we gather with our close friends and relatives to enjoy each other's company. This room can be comfortable and informal, but nevertheless it should be neat and clean, and in good order.

This room, more than the others, usually becomes the area where our family life is built and where most of our family memories are created. A Feng Shui consultant will generally suggest placing this area in one of the building's most favorable energy areas so that it optimally enhances the family life.

Shape

It is important for the previously mentioned rooms to have a regular shape, ideally square or rectangular, and to avoid diagonal walls that may cut the rooms into triangular or trapezoidal shapes. The best time to adjust uneven shapes is during a remodeling. They can be divided into separate areas, or corrected by installing built-ins that help camouflage the uneven walls. In some circumstances, mirrors can be used to create an illusory effect, but I personally do not like overdoing this technique because of the dynamic that it may create by interacting with the building's Invisible Qi, which may lead to less beneficial results.

The shape of the ceiling is also important. It can create a sense of ease if complicated features such as beams or uneven panels are avoided, particularly in the family room, where you may expect to spend more time than in the dining or living rooms.

These suggestions on how to correct the shape of rooms and ceilings apply mostly to all the important rooms of the house.

Furniture and Decoration

Rooms should be well kept, organized, and pleasantly decorated to make us and our guests feel comfortable. Colors and materials, which should be appropriate to the building's energy, should contribute to create balance and harmony.

Although cluttered communal rooms can make us feel overwhelmed and obstruct the Qi flow, the furniture and decoration should not be sparse so as to create a feeling of incompleteness.

As previously stated, be mindful not to overdo the use of antique furniture, especially in the living and dining room, which may be the more formal areas and perhaps used a little less. The Yin Qi built up by little use can be increased by the antique furniture, at the risk of making those rooms cold and uninviting.

These communal rooms should have at least a small open view to the outside and they should receive direct sunlight and air from the outside. Light and shade should also be well balanced in the room in terms of Yin and Yang. It is always preferable to have good sources of natural light and air in the room during the day.

Most of these suggestions regarding furniture and decorations can be applied to all the rooms in the house.

The Kitchen

The kitchen is an essential part of the house in Feng Shui, but is often overlooked. In the old days, it was considered a private part of the house, devoted exclusively to food preparation and not a place for socializing or entertaining. The kitchen thus was relegated to the rear of the house, and its door remained closed to guests at all times in order to hide the various functional activities that take place there.

Lifestyle habits have changed over time, and today the kitchen is more and more a vital part of the house, often open to the family room where guests socialize with hosts during food preparation. Nevertheless, food preparation remains the central focus of the kitchen. Such a vital life-giving aspect of our lives has specific Feng Shui rules in order to ensure our well being and maintain balance in the entire house.

The first of all the rules pertaining to the kitchen is to remember that the energy you embody while preparing food stays with it and is absorbed by the people eating that food. (This concept is echoed throughout many indigenous belief systems, including American Indian cultures.) Therefore, you may want to think twice before you start cooking if you are angry, unhappy, or preoccupied. In the same vein, it is not a good idea to bring emotional battles into the kitchen. This practice will spoil the Qi of your food. It is important to ensure that you are in a clear-minded, serene mood before you start playing with those pots!

Layout

To the majority of Feng Shui consultants, the kitchen is considered a private section of the house which should not be visible from the entry door or from the living room area, specifically since the food preparation and all the related activity may allow for it to not be clean and neat at all times. When working with limited space or when planning to use adjacent areas of a house for occasional entertainment, sliding doors or semi-transparent partitions can be used effectively to create separations.

It is important to maintain good air circulation in the kitchen so that cooking odors do not pollute the Qi in the rest of the house. Natural air circulation and natural light are preferable. Skylights can be added to increase both elements.

Avoid placing the stove and sink so that cooks must turn their backs to the door while working in the kitchen. The sudden appearance of an unexpected person may catch them by surprise, and they may hurt themselves while working.

The Stove

As a Feng Shui expert would typically indicate, the kitchen or stove should be placed in an area of the house with the least favorable Invisible Qi so that the fire used for the meal preparation will destroy any undesirable Qi collected in the house.

However, the stove should also be oriented in the most favorable direction, based on the building's energy, to receive the best Qi through which abundance and life-force energy can flow into the food.

In any case, the stove shouldn't be positioned in the path of the door. The entering Qi would then assault the stove rather than flow gently and this would have a disturbing effect.

In this kitchen layout, the stove and the sink are placed so that the cook can face the door of the kitchen and the sudden appearance of an unexpected person may not catch him or her by surprise (courtesy Snaidero USA).

It is advisable not to place the kitchen too close to any house entrance because the fire produced during meal preparation can burn the beneficial entering Qi.

It is popularly believed that the stove shouldn't be positioned opposite the sink, or immediately next to it, because the water element, embodied by the sink, will dominate the fire element, which is embodied by the stove. This belief is centuries old: in times past the water well resided in the kitchen and it was wise not to have it too close to the stove, where the food preparation may have possibly caused water pollution. In modern days, where both fire and water come out from pipes, this rule is not as pressing in terms of the harmony of the Feng Shui elements.

However, the modern counterpart, based primarily on functionality, is to have the different functions organized by elements: for example, have the dishwasher near by the sink, so that the "water functions" will all be grouped in one area. The same applies to the oven and stove top since they both belong to the fire element or functions.

In the kitchen layout, it is acceptable to have an oven and a stove top nearby, particularly if the kitchen size is small. However, a conflict will occur if water and fire objects are mixed, for example

187

a stove top on one side of the sink and the oven on the other, or a sink on one side of the stove and the dishwasher on the other. This layout tends to create confusion and uneasiness in the functional Qi of the room.

Windows and Skylights

Windows that are placed in immediate proximity to or behind a stove can dissipate the good Qi created while preparing the meal. Skylights have an upward movement that also directs the Qi toward the sky rather than around the stove where the cooking takes place. If, in order to bring natural light into the kitchen, a skylight is your only option, be mindful not to place it right above the stove.

Master Bedrooms, Children's and Guest Bedrooms

The bedroom is one of the most important areas of the house. The fact that we spend at least eight hours a day there is enough to indicate the huge impact it can have on us. Poor sleep, especially if chronic, makes us run down and irritable; our ability to manage stress becomes weak, and we become more susceptible to sickness and accidents.

Conversely, sound, regular sleep "recharges our batteries" and makes us more capable of counteracting stressful situations. Our immune systems remain strong, and we preserve our health. When we wake up refreshed, we are better able to work and to make decisions with clarity and alertness; this makes it easier to achieve success.

The purpose of the bedroom, to quote Frank Lloyd Wright, is primarily "to sleep and make babies." Multipurpose rooms with studios and offices do not really serve either of these purposes well. Additionally, a spouse may complain that you bring too much work into the relationship. In my experience, this kind of activity conflicts with the primary purpose of the room, and people often end up having neither refreshing sleep nor effective work time.

When consulting with an expert, you may be advised to orient a bed in a very specific direction, to place a bed in a certain spot in a room, or to locate the master bedroom in a specific area of the building based on the most favorable influences of the Invisible Qi. You may even be encouraged to design an entire bedroom around the bed location, based on the building's energy and the person's date of birth. This is a very crucial part of Feng Shui, and its effectiveness is very great. It is often worth customizing an entire building for this purpose alone.

When you do not know what the invisible influences are, the next best thing is to use appropriately beneficial design features, decorations, and colors to create comfortable and supportive sleeping quarters.

Shape

It is important to have a regular-shaped room, preferably square or rectangular. Avoid irregularly shaped, triangular or round rooms, since they cause unstable Qi patterns that can make your sleep restless. Rooms with "dead corners" and L or U shapes are not very favorable because the angles may create a stagnation in the Qi that will affect the entire room. It is preferable in this case to create a separate "sitting-room and retreat" area and to create a division between this section and the sleeping area.

Doors and Windows

It is preferable to have a limited number of openings to the room, only one entry door and all openings should offer the option to be closed (no door frames without doors). Numerous openings cause the benevolent Qi to be dispersed rather than contained, which will not contribute to well-being or to restful sleep.

Too many windows may have the same effect as doors, especially if large and if aligned with the entry door. It is advisable to have curtains or blinds that can be closed, especially at night, to help retain the Qi in the room.

The entry door to the bedroom shouldn't overlook descending

stairs because this will cause the Qi to flow away from the room. A flat area in front of the door is advisable to lead the Qi into the room.

Window placement is crucial in the bedroom. The room should be well lit, preferably by natural sunlight. Good ventilation is also essential; the room should be free from all odors. Stuffy rooms should be avoided, as the Qi tends to stagnate, affecting our health negatively.

Lighting

According to the Yin/Yang principles, the bedroom should not be very dark or overly bright. If too dark, it will promote Yin Qi and the stagnation of energy, while if too bright a room will have too much Yang energy, which will not promote restful sleep.

When possible, it is preferable for bedrooms to receive the Qi from the morning sun through at least one window. The vibrant Qi of the sun has Yang characteristics that, when lighting a room in the morning, can energize the room and its occupants, providing them with good Qi throughout the day.

Design Features

It is inadvisable to have ceiling beams in bedroom ceilings. Their heavy, imposing energy creates "pressure waves" over the body, making rest more difficult. In the long run, this can cause health problems and/or relationship difficulties. The same can be said for any object hanging from the ceiling; chandeliers, fans, and other such objects create disturbances in the pattern of Qi. It is preferable to have standing floor lamps radiating light onto the ceiling, which is then reflected down into the room, rather than heavy lighting fixtures, particularly above beds.

There should be no mirrors in the bedroom itself, particularly facing the bed. Mirrors reflect light. Since light carries Qi, then the mirror reflects the Qi along with the light and creates uneven patterns of Qi in the room, disturbing the natural flow. This could lead to sleeping disorders. The ideal position for a mirror is inside the closet door or in the adjacent bathroom.

Avoid sharp corners pointing toward the entry of the bedroom or toward the bed. This creates Sha energy, also called "poisoned arrow," which is not healthful.

Bed-location Do's and Don'ts

It is better to place a bed so that our feet do not point straight at the door. To have a door facing the bed, but out of direct alignment with the bed is acceptable.

It is advisable to have the headboard of the bed against a solid wall and not free-standing in the middle of the room.

A bed headboard tilted at a 45-degree angle to a corner is not very favorable because since the head is not supported, sleep may not be as restful. However, a solid headboard with a triangular filler, perhaps a furniture piece to fill up the corner can be used as countermeasure.

A glass wall, especially if facing the outdoors, does not constitute a sufficiently solid wall. The sleeping person's Qi will be attracted to the glass wall and will therefore not flow harmoniously through the body. In this case, a curtain can be used to give the glass wall a different effect: visually it will look solid and it will therefore no longer attract the Qi.

Colors

The colors and materials in a room should be chosen according to the personal energy of the occupants. However, the priority should be to first identify the building's energy and to introduce the necessary colors and elements to balance it, in accordance with professional Feng Shui advice.

In general, the décor should be harmonious and soft in colors and shades. This will create a suitable atmosphere that will help the sleepers relax and maintain quiet minds and bodies.

Exposed structural and decorative beams are very popular and valued design features. In a bedroom, however, they can cause relationship or health problems. It is preferable have a flat, unbroken ceiling overhead while sleeping (courtesy Move Italia).

A bed placed in the center of a bedroom may cause irregular sleep patterns, since the Qi flow is particularly active in the middle of a room. Also, a glass wall will not retain the Qi sufficiently, making the energy pattern of a room unstable (courtesy Move Italia).

Case Study: L. A. Designer

Since the energy moves much faster in the middle of the room, a bed positioned there will not be conducive to a comfortable sleep; the continuous Qi movement will keep the sleepers from resting well.

Years ago I consulted with a well-known local interior designer about her own apartment in Los Angeles. The design of the entire house, and of the bedroom in particular, was striking and extremely comfortable. However, something was amiss.

"I have such a hard time sleeping," she complained, "and worst of all I can hear every noise, and everything makes me so upset and stressed that I am seriously thinking of moving out. But I like this place so much . . . ."

After analyzing the apartment, I realized that there was nothing

A bed's headboard should be adjacent to a solid wall. If placed under a window, there may be Qi depletion through the opening and a consequent lack of restful sleep (courtesy Move Italia).

seriously wrong with the building's energy; only a few adjustments were necessary to balance it.

Since she had placed her bed right in the middle of the room, I asked her if she had ever tried sleeping with her headboard against the wall, and she told me that she had tried, but that that position had lead to frequent nightmares. That position had been Northwest (Qian-Metal): the worst possible direction for her personal energy type (Sun-Wood). So what she experienced made sense.

Our choices were limited, since there was a windowed wall, and the door to the bedroom and the doors to the closet and master bathroom intersected the other two walls. I therefore suggested she move the bed against the windowed wall. I also advised she add curtains across the wall to create a more solid feeling. This was her best sleeping direction, Southeast. It created a nice design look with the French window as headboard, but most importantly, her sleep improved dramatically. As a result, her tolerance for noise and stress also improved. About a year later her apartment was published in the *Los Angeles Times* magazine. To the reporter, she commented: "The (Feng Shui) changes have helped me to have peace of mind."

Irregular or slanted ceilings are not favorable in a bedroom. In the majority of cases, the bed should not be placed on the side where the ceiling is lower. Skylights are not recommended in bedrooms, particularly above the bed. Also, it is preferable not to squeeze the bed into a corner, but to allow an even distance from the adjacent walls and furniture on three sides. The desk in a child's room should be placed facing outward with the back against a solid wall to promote better concentration and study habits (courtesy Move Italia).

Children's Rooms

The overall design features that are recommended for an adult room can also be used for childrens' rooms. However, it is helpful to remember that children are a lot more Yang in their energy than the average adult; they thrive on learning, exploring, and being adventurous and their rooms may therefore need more color and stronger light.

Most of the time, parents decide what is best for the children, and this is often based on the parents' energy and needs, not necessarily the children's. A child's room should contain the things they like without the area around the bed becoming cramped with toys and other clutter.

I have often noticed that in contemporary living, the rooms

tend to get smaller and smaller and yet more multifunctional. Often the children's rooms become their study areas when they begin school. As we said for adults, mixing these two functions is not really appropriate. Children should learn at this early age to separate work from rest. As a parent, consider locating the study in a separate, adjacent room or in a separate section of the bedroom that is clearly defined as not being part of the sleeping area.

Nowadays a study area means finding a place for a computer, as well. This may be a really good time to consider delegating a separate area of the house as a computer-study room, since having electric and electronic appliances that create strong Fire Sha, or manmade electromagnetic fields, around a bedroom is not optimal.

The same may be said for TVs, alarm clocks, and elaborate stereo equipment.

When planning a new house, you may want to consider these possibilities ahead of time. A child may be only five years old now and may need only a twin bed and a play area, but in a few years, he or she may sleep more comfortably in a queen size bed and need a study area to do computer homework or to study with friends.

Guest Rooms

The guest room is generally a seldom-used area, unless we have frequent visitors or we use the room for other activities such as a home-office. If used only for guests visiting for a limited amount of time, such a room can be placed anywhere in the house, at your convenience, after determining the placement of other higher priority areas.

If designing the room for long term guests–perhaps members of the family spending months at a time–the room should be planned more carefully. In this case an expert would recommend a more favorable area based on the building's energy.

Generally speaking, because such a room is not used often it may tend to build up stagnant Qi over time. When expecting a guest, it is then advisable to freshen it up; open the windows, and let fresh air and sun do most of the work; use fresh bed linens and make the room warm and comfortable.

Bathrooms

Bathrooms, for obvious reasons, are the most private parts of the house and as such should be kept away (or at least not immediately visible) from social areas such as the living room, dining room, main entry, and the area immediately facing a staircase. This is one of the few rooms of the house that doesn't have to be placed in a good prosperity area, since the elimination of waste will disperse the beneficial influence of the Invisible Qi.

It is always preferable to have a real window in a bathroom rather than a "blind" one. A lack of fresh air and sunlight will cause Qi stagnation. That can be a problem if, for the purpose of air circulation, the door is left open and the stagnant and polluted Qi leaks into other rooms.

Toilet Placement

If we are designing a new bathroom, it is preferable to locate the toilet where it is not immediately visible when entering the room—preferably in a separate niche, in a partitioned area, behind a dividing wall or in a separate room. It is also a good rule to keep the door closed and the toilet seat down when not in use.

Garages, Storage, and Utility Rooms

While we do not spend a significant amount of our time in garages and storage or utility rooms, we should keep them well organized and clean at all times.

It is preferable to have the entrance from the garage that leads to the house near the main entrance area. The use of this secondary entrance will activate the energy flowing into that quadrant of the building as much as the main entrance would.

Since storage and utility rooms create separations and dampen sound, they are considered to be effective buffers between rooms and are therefore good transition spaces between garages and the main house. Garages, storage and utility rooms should not be immediately visible from the main entrance or from the formal living quarters.

Chapter 11

INTRODUCTION TO ADVANCED FENG SHUI THEORIES

The Feng Shui material we have covered so far deals mostly with the Visible Qi. This information is crucial when designing a building. Most of these teachings are very practical and easy to both visualize and apply. We have also covered the importance of house orientation, which determines its subtle energy and therefore the colors and materials that should be used. In this chapter, I would like to take you one step further into the more complicated areas of Feng Shui.

When entering the realm of advanced Feng Shui, some concepts can become much more complex. In fact, advanced Feng Shui deals mostly with the Invisible Qi, or "unseen influences." These higher-level teachings involve the study and application of theories such as the Eight Mansions (*Ba Zai Ming Jin*) and Flying Stars (*Xuan Kong*). They also involve the knowledge of gravesite location (*Yin Feng Shui*), I Ching (*Yi Jing*), Observing Things and Seeing Through the Obscure (*Guang Wu Dong Xuan Ge*), Three Kind of Trigrams (*San Ba Gua*), The Secret Five Ghosts (*Wu Gui*), Time Selection, Four Pillars of Destiny (Tzi Pei), Destiny Analysis (*Tzi Wei Dou Shu*), Palm and Face reading, and several other theories.

To further expand on all of these theories would require a lot of explanation and many practical examples. Most of all, these studies require much dedication, personal time, and natural talent. For the majority of students, it is crucial to study advanced Feng Shui under the guidance and supervision of an expert, rather than

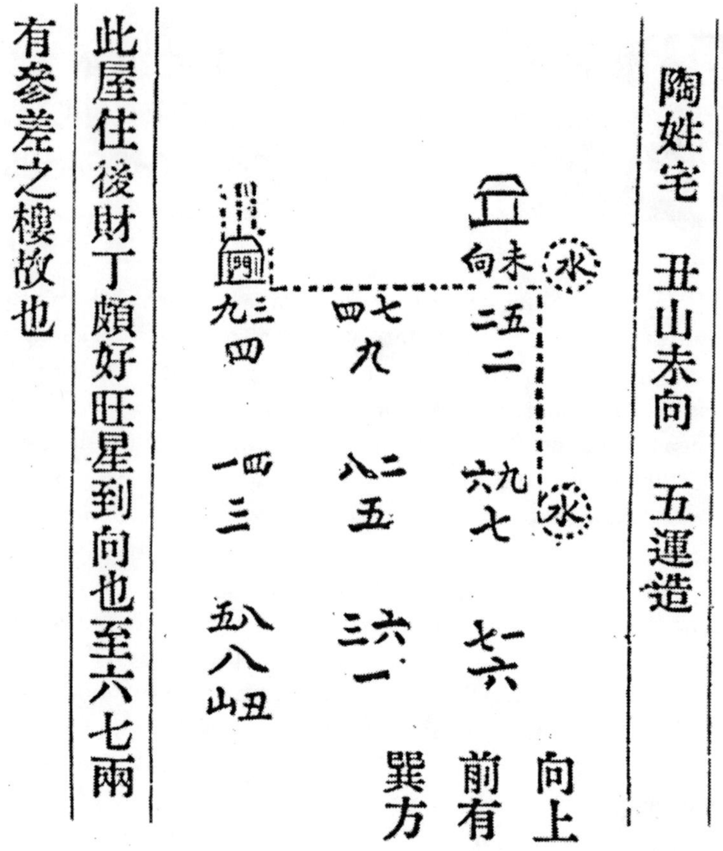

陶姓宅　丑山未向　五運造

向未　㊢（水）

九三　四七　二五二

九四　四九　六九七　㊢（水）

一四三　八二五　七六

五八丑　三六一　向上

　　　　巽方　前有

此屋住後財丁頗好旺星到向也至六七兩

有參差之樓故也

Case study of a building analyzed in *Master Shen's Xuan Kong Study (Shen Shi Xuan Kong Xue)* Tang Dynasty, 600-900 C.E. The nine sequences of three characters each comprise the Flying Stars combination (Xuan Kong System), while the character in the broken-line circle, *shui*, is the Chinese word for water.

only by reading literature. Often, the experience that an expert can contribute is worth ten thousand words.

Many of these theories deal with the effects of the Invisible Qi on individuals. They examine minute changes in the life-force energy of the Cosmos, Earth's response to it, and how people, based on their unique life-force frequencies, relate to it.

The Effects of Time and Qi Changes

The effects of time on Qi changes are like a chemical process in which small particles of the life—force energy of the universe can affect the delicate balance of the Qi in every building, mixing with the building's energy and creating or destroying according to each building's potential.

For example: The Xuan Kong System incorporates the time variable (year, month, day, hour, etc.) into the Five Elements, Yin and Yang and Eight Trigrams theories.

As we have seen earlier, a house located on a Southwest-Northeast axis belongs to the Earth element and according to the Five Elements Theory (see Chapter 4), Earth is supported by Fire. Therefore a Fire element year enhances the house's energy. Let's suppose that the following year is an Earth element year. What will happen to our house? That year's energy will also be potentially favorable, because Earth supports itself in the Five Elements Theory.

As a result, during the Fire and Earth years the building will be at its best, consequently, the occupants will match the active potential of the building just by living in it. They will prosper, accomplish many of their endeavors with ease, and enjoy overall well being.

Now let's say, a few years later, a Wood-energy year comes around and since Wood dominates Earth, that year's energy will dominate the energy of the house, leaving its energy weaker than it was during the Fire and Earth years. A similar weakening of the energy will occur when Metal years come around, since Metal drains from the Earth's Energy.

During those years, the occupants, who are still matching the energy of the building, will find themselves living with a less supportive energy and they will have to work harder to achieve their goals.

This simple example helps us understand how the Invisible Qi of time affects the building's energy and how it impacts the lives of the occupants. Theoretically, every building in the world is subject to these changes because they all relate to the time changes of Qi in the environment around us, yet some buildings may be more affected than others, both in terms of positive and negative outcomes. Why so?

About thirty percent of negative effects can be attributed to a poor flow of Visible Qi around the building. With the help of this book, you can walk around and inside a building and spot all the potential sources of stagnant Qi or features that could deplete the building's energy. Buildings with several of these unhealthy characteristics tend to be more adversely affected by the element of time. By implementing the suggestions in this book, you'll be able to correct or counteract the majority of these situations. The remaining factors have to do with the building's energy and how it relates to its occupants. This is the realm of Invisible Qi.

A Building's Energy

Once the roof is constructed, the energy of the environment, which incorporates both time and orientation, is sealed inside and becomes the energy of the building. The building's energy starts aging immediately after construction is completed, which wouldn't have happened had the energy not been sealed. Therefore, the location of the building, its exact orientation (to the degree), the date of construction, and its internal energy distribution all come together in determining the building's specific energy. I like to refer to this as a building's DNA or genetic code: a unique composition of factors that combine the energy from heaven or the cosmos (*Tai Yang*, the Big Father) with the energy from Earth (*Tai Yin*, the Big Mother).

Each building will be completely different from the next, unless

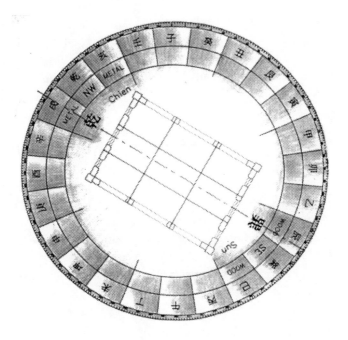

The invisible, internal energy pattern and layout of a building can be altered dramatically according to its orientation. This effect is particularly evident as it pertains to the date of construction of each building. The help of a Feng Shui expert at an advanced level is advisable to help distinguish a favorable building orientation from one that is unfavorable.

built in the same time, with the same orientation, and with the same internal layout. This means that in a neighborhood where buildings are all different from one other and where some may have been built earlier and some later, each building will have different internal energy characteristics and should, therefore, be analyzed separately.

On the other hand, let's consider a new development where houses are built around a cul-de-sac. Although the buildings were probably built at the same time, each of them will be facing a different orientation due to the round shape of the cul-de-sac. Although all the buildings may look the same and may be designed alike both in their exterior and interior layouts, the internal energetic characteristics of those buildings are going to be completely different; a one-degree difference in the orientation can make a building's energy distribution completely different from the one next to it. In such a case, only a well-trained expert can distinguish their qualities and the necessary corrections or improvements that may be required.

A Building's Energy and Internal Layout Design

The Feng Shui characteristics of houses are greatly affected by their internal layouts. For example, a house built in the year 2003 (A) along a SW-NE axis (facing southwest between 217.5 and 232.5 degrees) is going to provide the potential for creativity and fame. However, if the same house were to be built in 2004 (B) with the same orientation, it would have the potential to promote pain and sickness.

In House A, in order to support the career achievement of the occupants, the best location for the master bedroom would be in the western quadrant. A red color element could be added to the room to further increase this favorable potential. In this case, red would also be in harmony with the natural Earth energy of the house, as seen in previous chapters.

In House B, although it has the same orientation, the western quadrant has a very different potential, it is particularly unfavorable for women owners and it would therefore not be the best location for a master bedroom, especially if occupied by a woman. It would be preferable to use this area for a master closet or bathroom instead and as far as the master bedroom is concerned, it would be better to pick the southeast location, which has the potential to promote creativity, spirituality, and romance. Although the use of the color red would theoretically be appropriate for this building, in this particular location this color should be limited or avoided, since it has the potential to further exacerbate the unfavorable potential of this area. The water element in this case is preferable.

The energy distribution in a building is fairly territorial, and to place a bed in the west or in the southeast, in our case, will make a major difference based purely on the time of construction of the building. To design a building built in 2003 meant to design a floor plan completely different than if the same building were to be built in 2004.

The same is true if a room is in the north, south, east, southeast, southwest or northeast. In other words, each direction is going to have a different energy component, and each house will be different.

The "life station" system used in some Western adaptations of Feng Shui assigns the same potential to each direction in every building. This is a simplistic, cookie-cutter approach and in advanced Feng Shui we recognize that it cannot truly be accepted as accurate.

Existing Buildings, New Projects, and Remodeling

An advanced Feng Shui analysis becomes critical when planning a new building and deciding which orientation would have the best potential taking into account the time frame during which we intend to build it. Most important, planning from the beginning using advanced Feng Shui Architectural principles allows us to design an interior layout that places the most important activity spaces (i.e., places where we spend most of our time) in the most favorable energy areas of the building.

In existing buildings where advanced Feng Shui architecture concerns were not taken into consideration before construction, rooms are often placed relatively randomly, and there is generally less than a fifteen-percent chance that some of them will actually coincide with the building's favorable energy areas.

Although correcting pre-existing building conditions can be more convenient in terms of cost or time, according to Feng Shui, it is much more beneficial to address a building's energy considerations in the planning stages, so as to achieve the most effective results overall. During a remodeling process, such corrections can also be introduced very effectively, especially when the remodeling involves some structural changes.

Needless to say, these projects are much more complex than the evaluation of an existing building and they therefore require the competence of an expert Feng Shui consultant with experience in both architecture and interior planning, who can also communicate effectively with both the architects and the designers involved in the project.

Matching Occupants and Buildings

Last but not least, I would like to dedicate a few words about the Eight Mansions Theory, which addresses the compatibility between buildings and people and the effect this has on their lives. This identifies people's individual energy and determines their own basic orientation in space. To a certain extent, this determines the compatibility between people and their homes.

For example, as we have seen earlier, a building that sits northeast and faces southwest belongs to the Earth element. The people who will be most compatible with this building are people who, based on their dates of birth, also belong to either the Earth or Metal element. However, people whose energy is associated with the Water element will feel overpowered by the house's energy (Earth stops the Water from flowing), while people who belong to the Fire element may feel drained by an Earth house.

There are also a few other advanced Feng Shui factors to take into account in considering the compatibility between buildings and people:

- the most favorable sleeping direction
- secondary or alternative sleeping directions
- the best entry direction
- alternative favorable entry directions
- the most favorable sections of the house for a person's energy

The Eight Mansions Theory focuses on the orientation of the person in the building's space. Since it deals with the directions of the energy of this planet as they relate to the magnetic north, imbalances cannot be effectively remedied with colors or materials, but only by modifying the orientation of the building or of the interior design.

This theory does not involve the time factor and to a certain extent, it may appear to be in conflict with other advanced theories; however, a qualified expert will evaluate all of them when performing an analysis and will know when one takes priority over another.

Conclusion

I believe my clients when they tell me that when they first entered a house they felt either very comfortable or uncomfortable; this is a natural reaction, on a physical level, to the Visible Qi.

In this book you have learned how to "read" the flow of the Visible Qi of the surrounding environment and inside a building. You now have an extensive checklist of landscape and design features to help you enhance or correct the natural Qi flow so that a building and its residents will benefit from it at all times. This information can also serve you in a pre-purchase examination so that you can determine the potential of a building before taking the next step and purchasing it.

When deciding to embark on a more complex project, you may find yourself in need of some additional help from a professional Feng Shui architect. The information in this book will help you evaluate the skills and the credibility of an expert should you decide to hire one. Remember, qualified Feng Shui experts are rare and hard to find, but the right one can make a world of a difference. I therefore strongly recommend that you invest some serious time toward finding the right Feng Shui expert for you and your home.

Good luck in your Feng Shui adventures!

SIMONA F. MAININI, Dr. Arch.

Combining Italian design and ancient Asian wisdom, Simona Mainini has found the perfect balance for living in harmony with the forces of nature. Her unique approach to uniting good design, functionality, and the natural environment derives from a strong background in the arts and design. She is a licensed architect in Italy and holds a Doctor in Architecture degree from the Politecnico di Milano and a diploma from the School of Arts of Reggio Emilia, Italy. She studied Traditional Feng Shui with Master 'Sifu' Lawrence Sang. She is currently a senior instructor for the American Feng Shui Institute and also teaches at UCLA.

Dr. Mainini's family business, Mainini Arreda e Illumina, specializes in luxury interior design and Italian furnishings and is the only such firm in Italy offering full-service Traditional Feng Shui consultation. In October of 1999, she presented the full-scale *Italian Feng Shui House* at the Exhibition Center in Reggio Emilia, Italy.

In 1997, Dr. Mainini established Feng Shui Architecture, Inc., an international consulting firm specializing in Feng Shui applications, to promote the integration of the ancient science with current design trends in modern and traditional architecture. Her knowledge and skills have contributed to helping many homeowners and business owners improve their environments through the use of feng shui principles. She has also consulted for well-known international corporations, diplomats, and celebrities both in the U.S. and in Italy, as well as with architectural and interior design firms interested in bringing the advantages of Feng Shui to their clients.

Reviews of Dr. Mainini's projects have appeared in the *Los Angeles Times Magazine* (July 12, 1998), in the Italian magazines

Casaviva (October, 1999), *GdA International* (July, 1999), *GdA Italy* (September, 1999), *Casa Idea* (February, 2000), *Tra Terra e Cielo* (February, 2000), and *Report Casa & Natura* (January-March, 2000), as well as in *Feng Shui for Modern Living* (August, 2000), *Brentwood Magazine* (Sept-Oct., 2000), *Donna Moderna* (February, 2001), and *The Orange County Register* (June 2001-April 2002). Her works are also featured in Dr. Carol Soucek King's book *Feng Shui at Home* (May, 1999). She also wrote a monthly column for *Sport & Fitness*, an Italian-language magazine specializing in well-being and healthy lifestyles.

Dr. Mainini offers lectures, classes, and seminars for professionals and nonprofessionals, both in the U.S. and abroad, through UCLA Extension, the American Institute of Architects (AIA), the Building Industry Association, Westweek, Neocon West, the International Furniture Exhibition in Milan, and International Feng Shui Conferences.

Speakers at the Feng Shui World Congress, 2000. First row, from the left: Prof. Thomas Lin Yun, Dr. Arch. Simona Mainini, Master Jap Chen Hai (Singapore), Jami Lin, Master Raymond Lo (Hong Kong).

Simona Mainini is a member of the American Feng Shui Society. She lives in Beverly Hills, California, where her firm is based. Her Web site can be found at www.fengshuiarch.com

Contact Us

We hope you have enjoyed reading this book. We would greatly appreciate your feedback. Please fill in the following information and mail it to our address:

FENG SHUI ARCHITECTURE, Inc.
287 S. Robertson Blvd., Suite 398
Beverly Hills, CA 90211 USA
Tel: 310 860 8989-310 772 8188

Name: _____

Address: _____

_____

Tel.: _____ E-mail address: _____

Date of Birth: _____ Occupation: _____

Your comments on this book:

_____

_____

_____

_____

_____

_____

Are you interested in a consultation for your home or business? Please contact our Beverly Hills office at 310 860 8989

Would you like to receive our e-mail newsletter? If yes, please enter e-mail address

_____

*Personal information contained in this form are strictly for Feng Shui Architecture survey and promotions.

Disclaimer

The information offered in this book is to the author's best knowledge and experiences and makes no claims for absolute effectiveness. It can be beneficial or harmful, depending upon one's stage of development. Readers should use their own discretion and liability. The adoption and application of the material offered in this book remains solely the reader's own responsibility. The author, publisher, dealers, distributors or representatives of this book are not responsible or liable in any manner for loss or damage of properties or bodily injuries that may occur by following the instructions in this book.

Anecdotes contained in this book are real, although names have been changed to protects clients privacy.

Printed in the United States
108406LV00002B/70/A